The Homestead

a memoir

SYLVIE GRAYSON

For information contact:

GREAT WESTERN PUBLISHING at
sylviegraysonauthor@gmail.com

For information contact
sylviegraysonauthor@gmail.com
www.sylviegrayson.com

ISBN: 978-1-989491-11-9

Great Western Publishing is a registered trademark of Sylvie Grayson.

Book Cover – Created by Steven Novak, novakillustration@gmail.com from an old family photo of our home.

Other books by Sylvie Grayson

Contemporary romantic suspense
Suspended Animation
Legal Obstruction
The Lies He Told Me, Book One
Rain Man, Lies Book Two
Don't Move, Lies Book Three
Game Plan, Lies Book Four
My Best Mistake
False Confession
Dead Wrong
Woodland Pursuit

Historical
Prairie Storm
Moon Shine
The Homestead

Sci-fi/fantasy

Aqatain, The Last War: Prequel
Khandarken Rising, The Last War: Book One
Son of the Emperor, The Last War: Book Two
Truth and Treachery, The Last War: Book Three
Weapon of Tyrant, The Last War, Book Four
Prince of Jiran, The Last War: Book Five
Banderos, The Last War: Book Six
The Sovereign, The Last War: Book Seven

Praise for Sylvie Grayson's books

I've been reading Sylvie Grayson's books - can't seem to put them down. How do you come up with these exciting mysteries? Very fun reading!!

Suspended Animation

Wow! This book is amazing, its very well written and the characters are very well developed. This is my first book by Sylvie Grayson and it won't be my last. I was hooked from the first page and it was very hard to put down.

Interesting characters, family conflicts and divided loyalties make this a book that kept me up half the night

Legal Obstruction

I loved this book! I've found my new favorite author.

Emily is a fiercely professional woman who is on her own and determined to protect her little family. Joe is a solitary guy who often doesn't deal with problems until they are front and center. But boy does Emily wake him up and does he take notice. Add in a wildcard assistant and a few unsavory characters and I was up all night finishing the book to find out what happens.

The Lies He Told Me

If you are a fan of the heartwarming craftiness and domesticity of a Debbie McComber romance, and the intense intrigues of Danielle Steele, you'll enjoy the writing style of Sylvie Grayson; where the bad guys are not heartless, and the good guys are virtually flawless.

Khandarken Rising, The Last War: Book One

The General of Khandarken sends his son, Dante, to investigate the situation. When Dante meets the lovely Beth she eyes him with suspicion. But he won't stop until he solves the tangle of motives, fueled by greed, which threaten Beth and her family. I enjoyed this book very much. The well-developed characters and sensuous love scenes make this a page turner. I look forward to reading Book Two and Book Three

… this story is one of a kind in its own and couldn't be truly compared to anything but itself. It has so many unique characteristics to it. The personal relationships are intriguing and different from many other fictional relationships. The names are cool, the plot gets thicker with each page, and I loved the author's style. It became evident that I was addicted to reading it and was sad to be finished. I'm going to give this a strong recommendation. It's my kind of book.

Son of the Emperor, The Last War: Book Two

I am a big fan of The Last War series. I loved Book One, the story of Major Dante Regiment and Beth Farmer. The dystopian world Grayson has created, where women are scarce and Clones are used to replace them, where the Emperor has finally been defeated but his son takes up the fight, just gets better in this second book. …Thrills abound on the race to freedom and home. I really enjoyed this book and can't wait for Book Three. Grayson has great imagination, the fantasy series is awesome.

Truth and Treachery, The Last War: Book Three - Ok, this series is just getting better and better. The increasing complexity of the characters and the development of lead characters is a pleasure to read. The plot, with its twists and turns, intrigue and adventure, is a real joy. If you liked the first two books in The Last War series (and, seriously, that's the place to start before reading this book - it's worth doing) then you will love this book.

Weapon of Tyrants, The Last War: Book Four

The Last War has been a truly excellent series so far, and Weapon of Tyrants is staying strong. Exciting, full of intrigue and adventure, wonderfully developed strong lead characters with a great supporting cast, neat world-building and excellent writing. I mean, what more can you ask for? You do need to start with book 1 in this series, but it too was excellent so you can't go wrong, and I can guarantee you'll have a ball with this one when you reach it.

Prince of Jiran, The Last War: Book Five

I was surprised and completely enthralled! I haven't read a book like this ever. I could not put it down. You fall in love with Prince Shandro and Princess Chinata who against all odds fall in love. Their long journey and the difficulties with Judson set this apart from most other books. This is a book you'll love and have to read from beginning to end without putting it down!. Very highly recommended!

Banderos, The Last War: Book Six

As with the other five novels in the Last War series, the descriptive narratives of their world, and of the characters and their family groups are terrific. Each of these can be read as a Stand Alone with a HEA! However, there are so many fine characters that build upon their inter-relationships, I urge you to start with the first book and read each one successively, as I have done. I was hooked with the first story.

THE HOMESTEAD

THE HOMESTEAD

DEDICATION

This book is dedicated to my sisters and brothers who lived this adventure with me and survived to move on and live a normal life.

God bless you all.

Contents

THE HOMESTEAD

THE HOMESTEAD

This is the story of my family's adventure when I was a child. We left the Canadian west coast on Vancouver Island, British Columbia, travelled to the North Peace River area in the northern part of the province, established our home there by claiming some homestead land, and then, years later, we left. It is the story of six children who managed to live this adventure and build a new life after the journey ended. Here is how it happened.

FOREWORD
By Sylvie's husband, Brian

I have long urged Sylvie to write this book for several reasons. Firstly, because in this day and age a true pioneering story is rare, given the technology and development in our western world of North America. Secondly, her unique person needs to be explained to fully appreciate the depth of her character. And thirdly, the knowledge of her background lends credibility to the fabric of her storytelling. Believe me, she knows whereof she writes.

I met Sylvie on an evening out after a long work day. My business partner and I went to a live music bar and with a beer in hand I spied her at a table and asked her to dance. We danced and talked for a couple of hours, finding that we were both separated from long term marriages. I never dated or even looked at another woman from then on as I became incredibly aware of the depth and strength and the compatibility of her person with me.

As I read the chapters of The Homestead, I am so aware of the absolute and stark difference of Sylvie's adolescent years and university years to my own. Growing up in Montreal, I was blessed to have a very stable home life and was even able to walk to my university campus from my family home. My high school years were filled with socializing, weekend parties, ski and skating outings, baseball, football and hockey sports and student activities.

When I had a chance to see Sylvie's history and reflect on the chasm of difference in our separate development years, I had a deeper and deeper understanding and respect for the steel and strength of her person to have surmounted the challenges of her early years. And she not only surmounted but thrived at everything she undertook.

While I worked hard on the Montreal docks every summer to pay for my college tuition and books, it was nothing compared to Sylvie's situation. She was paying board at home and working two jobs through summer and winter to pay her way. Then she left home on her own to attend university in Victoria, again working day and night to support herself, sharing rental bedrooms and making do with what little she had. Her background did not break her, it made her able to tolerate the otherwise intolerable. But it did wound her, and she has suffered from chronic fatigue, likely as a result of lifelong stress. But even this she has worked diligently to overcome with every kind of intervention, never giving up or giving in.

When I wrote a short speech to celebrate her at a recent birthday, I said –

"Sylvie is a formidable woman. Capable of almost anything. Skilled in business, family, the kitchen, and life in general. She is unnervingly courageous and the ultimate pragmatist. Her reach does not exceed her grasp… ever. And … her grasp has an incredible reach!"

Enjoy this book.

It is not only a testament to her indomitable spirit, but also an uplifting tale of the human ability to make the most of the least.

HOMESTEADING

A homestead is defined as a home and land occupied by the person or family that claims it. But homesteading means something slightly different. In Canada, homesteading was a programme offered in the past by the government in many provinces with the goal of settling the land. There was also a drive to increase the population, often from outside the country, encouraging immigration.

In British Columbia, the government passed a new homesteading act which encouraged people to claim land in the 1950s and 1960s. The land was divided into sections, 640 acres each, and each section was divided into quarter sections of 160 acres. A section is measured as one mile by one mile in size, and a quarter section is a half mile by a half mile square.

The Land Titles office in each area had maps and a list of the land that was still available. Upon application, a person could claim a quarter section. Veterans from the Second World War were especially encouraged to apply. There were no taxes payable on the property until the settler managed to complete title transfer which was to occur within five years.

The goal was to move onto the land, build a home, and carry out developments or what were then called *improvements*. These could include clearing the land, planting crops and farming it, or building barns and raising animals, whatever was needed to become self-sufficient. The goal was to *improve* the land over a period of 5 years from the first claim. If the homesteader succeeded in doing that, they could then make application with proof of improvements, and the land title would be transferred into his or her name without payment.

Free land! But wait a minute, not quite free. Developing the land could be quite a challenge and incur substantial effort and expense, depending on where it was located and what the land was like. Was it heavily forested, or spread over steep hills? Was it a wetland, covered in sloughs and creeks which divided the area, or made it unfarmable? Was there a road providing access to the property or did you have to build your own road to get there? A lot of things could change the focus of how easy or expensive it was to obtain and keep the free land.

MY PARENTS – DAD

Thomas, Dad's grandfather, left England in 1857 and arrived by ship in Canada. He started out by claiming twenty acres of land in Upper Canada, now called Ontario. He married a young woman whose family was also from England, and built a log house on his land for the coming family. They had twelve children, six girls in a row, followed by six boys.

I have travelled to their home in Upper Canada and have seen the house. It was being used for storage by the current owner of the property at the time, but still stood on the land they had owned. The structure was tiny, likely had two rooms and a couple of windows, built of logs.

They weren't there too long, as the government opened up homesteading on the Canadian Prairies in the 1880's. They took their wagon, horses, and whatever assets they could carry that would be useful in their new home, and travelled across the prairies.

By this time, most of the girls had married, and some of them, with their husbands, travelled with Thomas and his family to settle the prairies. Two of the boys had died in their childhood, but the remaining four sons made the journey as well.

They all laid claim to land in southern Saskatchewan. The Land Titles Office had a problem, in that there were five men with the same last name claiming land in the same area. The father and one of the sons had the same first name as well. It was an issue that confused the clerks in the office and took a few years to clear up.

George, the twelfth child and youngest son, was my grandfather. George and his next older brother, the eleventh child, married two sisters from their new home, a place called Sintaluta in southern Saskatchewan. George and his wife, Emily Annie Maria, proceeded to produce their own family. Dad was their seventh child, born on the family farm. When he was one and a half years old and his youngest brother was two months old, in February of 1919, Emily died of the Spanish flu that swept through in 1918 and 1919 after the end of World War I. George's mother, Hannah Ruth, my father's grandmother, died of the flu the following day, and the two funeral services were held together in the local village church. The women were buried side by side. Emily Annie's father fell ill at the same time as his daughter but he survived the illness.

According to one of my cousins who knew George, our grandfather was devastated by these losses, and more or less gave up. His youngest son was in need of a mother when his wife died. George's brother and his wife, Emily's sister, took over the raising of the baby. However, George continued to farm with his father and brothers. Each one of them had claimed land in the same area and they used their horses and equipment in a united effort to work the soil.

A couple of years later, snow came early to the Prairies. The family had harvested their father's crop and were working down the list of brothers from oldest to youngest. George, as the youngest brother, was last on the list and before they got to his fields the snow had flattened his crop, demolishing his total income for the year. Unable to pay his taxes, he lost his land. He took his family of motherless children by train, moving them to Nipawin, in northern Saskatchewan. He set up shop in the small town as a saw and knife sharpener.

As a consequence, Dad grew up motherless and more or less fatherless. He remembers sleeping with his sister on a mattress on the swept dirt floor in a tiny log cabin just outside the small town of Nipawin. One night he woke, terrified he was alone. But when he looked around, he saw an angel standing at the foot of the mattress, keeping guard over him. He was able to calm down and go back to sleep, secure in the knowledge that he was safe.

Dad was used to being without and used to being alone. At some point he discovered the lost brother, Lewis, the baby who had been born just a few months before his mother died. This made him one of eight children, not seven. The baby had remained with his aunt and uncle in Sintaluta when the rest of the family moved north.

My uncle, this younger brother, whom I met many years later, told me the story of how, as a child, he had found out who his parents really were. Sintaluta was a small town so everyone knew everyone else's business. He lived close enough to the village to attend the two-room elementary school there. One day when he was about ten, he'd had an altercation with another boy in the schoolyard and fists were flying. The other boy was angry and shouted at him, "You don't even know your own parents. Those people aren't your folks." He heard the words, but didn't understand what the boy was taunting him about. It took him a few days to sort it out in his mind, and work up the courage to ask his parents what it meant.

They sat him down and told him the truth—they were his aunt and uncle, not his physical mother and father. The other children in the family were his cousins, not his brothers and sisters as he'd assumed. "We meant to tell you. We knew we had to tell you," they said. "But it never seemed like the right time. In our hearts, you are our son."

My father and his younger brother met for the first time as teenagers, and came in contact again as young men during World War Two, my Dad in a navy uniform, his lost brother in army gear at the start of the war. When I finally met Uncle Lew, my father had already passed.

Lew recited the story of two brothers, each six feet tall, meeting up and wearing different military uniforms. But my father was five feet nine and a quarter inches tall according to his navy records. Lew had obviously been overwhelmed with meeting an older brother he hardly knew.

Dad's approach to being sick included working it off outside rather than giving in and going to bed.

When he got the flu, he worked in the fresh air, finding some physical labor to do, until he felt better. He told a story about feeling ill and having a fever as a young man while still living at home. So he went out and chopped firewood for his father. A family friend who was a medical doctor had come to visit at the house, and when he heard Dad didn't feel well and had a fever, he went out to check on him, diagnosing diphtheria. The doctor instructed Dad to attend the next day at his medical clinic to be vaccinated, as there had been a number of cases in the town.

MY PARENTS—MUM

Mum was raised in a family of seven children. Her parents were from England, her father, Sidney, from Southampton, her mother, Rosa, from Rye. The father's family ran a grocery store in Portsmouth, and Sidney joined the English navy at age nineteen.

A few years later, he resigned to sign up for the Royal Canadian Navy Volunteer Reserve, the precursor of the Canadian Navy, which was in the process of being formed, and travelled to Canada on the HMCS Rainbow. This vessel was the first ship of the Canadian navy, which had been purchased by Canada from Britain and landed at Esquimalt, Vancouver Island, British Columbia in 1910. He settled there and completed his service in the navy until retirement.

Rosa's family ran a pub and bakery in Folkestone, England, and she emigrated to Canada with her parents in about 1914, at the start of the First World War. Rosa and Sidney met in Esquimalt and married.

Mum was their third child, and when she was a young girl of ten years, she was devastated by the death of her brother, Arthur, two years younger than herself. They had been close, sharing a bed. He was run over in the street by a fuel delivery truck.

When I did a search on this event, I found the newspaper report of the memorial. The truck driver was actually a pall bearer at the funeral, clearly devastated by the accident. Apparently Arthur was playing kick ball with some friends, and ran into the street to retrieve the ball just as the truck rolled past.

The loss of her brother had a lasting effect on my mother's life. I remember she mourned for Arthur even as an adult.

She was raised to be polite, speak correctly, and always use her manners. She did needlework, could knit or sew anything, loved to paint pictures, and gardened for food and flowers. But especially her talent was with words, in both poetry and prose.

THE EARLY YEARS

My parents met in Esquimalt when Dad was sent from the Prairies to Vancouver Island for his training in the Canadian Navy. They married during the Second World War. After the war ended, they settled in Victoria, where my two older sisters, Pamela and Nell, were born. I was born there also.

We lived in a small house near the Gorge waterway. There we had a goat for milk. The animal ate everything in sight, even the ribbons from our hair and the hems of our dresses.

I remember getting a new pair of lace-up boots. I was thrilled with them and knew they enabled me run fast. Dad came out that evening to call us in for dinner, but I was too busy admiring my boots to pay attention. He came out again to look for me, drying his hands on a towel. He called me to come in and I just looked at him. I had never seen him run, and my new boots made me very fast. So instead of obeying, I took off across our yard. I heard him laugh behind me, and then within three strides he had me under his arm and took me into the house.

When I was five, our parents sold their small house in Victoria, situated near the Gorge waterway, and bought a box truck. Dad loaded all of our furnishings into the truck, positioning a couch in the front facing forward, with a window cut out of the box, allowing us to see through the windshield of the cab, and watch the road ahead during the trip. This is where my sisters and I travelled, looking through the front window as we drove across the Prairies.

We travelled east for weeks and ended up in Nipawin, northern Saskatchewan, Dad's old hometown. However, we weren't there long. Obviously things didn't work out as Dad had hoped they would, and about eight months after we arrived, we were riding in an old Ford car headed back to Vancouver Island. It was Christmas Eve when we stopped on our journey to overnight at a hotel in Regina, Saskatchewan. I remember running up and down the hallways on the second floor with my sisters, working off steam after a long day of travelling in the car.

There was an elderly bachelor in one of the hotel rooms who invited us in for a sip of pop and some candies. We never got pop, and were thoroughly excited to receive such a treat.

Once we arrived back on Vancouver Island, we stopped in the town of Duncan, just north of Victoria, and bought a house there. This house had three rooms, and was about five hundred and twenty square feet in size, with a front porch and a set of stairs at the back leading down to the yard. After about a year, Dad had enclosed the front porch to create an indoor bathroom with running water so we didn't have to run outside to use the outhouse. He then set about digging a new well in the yard as the old one was too shallow and ran out of water in the heat of summer.

This house did not have a foundation, so Dad set about creating one. He jacked up the whole structure, using car jacks. Then he dug troughs for the foundation, built wood frames and poured concrete into them. He added rocks to take up space and use less cement. He mixed the cement in the wheel barrow and slowly worked his way around the house, filling the foundation.

I was totally enthralled with watching his work. To have an indoor bathroom was wonderful, of course. But to raise the whole house and create a foundation was amazing to me. I used to follow him around, asking questions and making my own observations.

Next he built himself a workshop off to the side of the yard. Inside he set up his equipment—tape measures, levels, planes, chisels, vices, and so on. He did a lot of lathe work, making rocking chairs, coffee tables, bread boxes, carved plaques and statues.

I had watched him carve spindles with his lathe many times and when, about ten, I asked if I could try it. He said, "Sure." Dad handed me the chisel and turned on the machine. Almost immediately, he reached forward and turned it off again. My hair was hanging free and I had just leaned forward to take a closer look.

The fourth daughter, Cindy, was born in Duncan, as well as the first son, Derek.

I was a very quiet child, being a natural introvert. Third of four daughters, I had two older sisters who spoke for me when words were needed. My school teachers didn't always know what to make of me, one of them thought my sister next in line—who also didn't talk much but who was very fair, was in fact Dutch and didn't speak any English at all. However, there was an additional reason for our unwillingness to engage.

There was often a shortage of life's necessities at our house. Not only clothes and shoes as we outgrew what we had, but food was invariably in short supply. I know Mum often made a thin soup to stretch what she had to feed us, and when we balked at eating it, she used the strap to make us cooperate with her requests. She also said she was afraid of what would happen if the 'authorities' discovered the sparseness of our meals. She often repeated her instructions not to ever talk about what went on at home. She said she was concerned we would be taken away from our home and put into care. The comment sounded like a threat that I didn't completely understand.

Now, at six and seven years old, I didn't know what part of *what went on at home* was secret. Consequently, I didn't talk at all, ensuring I never divulged the wrong information.

I was so quiet that my first three teachers thought I was 'slow' in my work. Then I hit grade four. There, I had a wonderful teacher who saw through the silent child and into the brain that was working full tilt. She took me and another student to one side of the classroom and tutored us separately from the rest of the class for the last months of the school year. Mostly she worked on arithmetic and English. At the end of the year, we both passed into grade six, skipping grade five altogether.

Dad was a journeyman carpenter, able to perform just about any construction task. Upon his formal discharge from the navy, one of the comments of his commanding officer was 'Don is very good with his hands.' But in spite of his abilities, he somehow didn't fit the mold of a regular working man.

He took several carpenter jobs while in Duncan, one of them working on the construction of the Chemainus mill, but none of them lasted very long. After six years, Mum and Dad decided Duncan was a poor fit for our family and they had become interested in the homesteading land grant program in the North Peace River area of British Columbia.

OUR TRAVEL NORTH

Dad found an old pickup truck and cut the bed off. He welded a ball mount hitch onto the back frame of our car, and a towing hitch onto the front frame of the truck bed and attached it to the car. We loaded what would fit into the truck bed, including the crib, beds and linens.

Most of the bigger items, such as a full-sized pump organ and a washing machine were shipped by railroad to the north.

By now there were five children. Mum and Dad sat in the front seat of the car with our youngest sister, Cindy, positioned between them. We three older girls sat in the back, with our one-year-old brother, Derek. He crawled restlessly over our laps and legs during the entire voyage. I had no idea where we were going or where we would end up. But we had undertaken such journeys before so I was confident I would soon find out what awaited me at the end of this trip.

It is a long drive from Vancouver Island to the North Peace River area, especially in those days with the type of vehicle we had. Today, it is eight hundred and fifty miles or thirteen hundred and sixty kilometres by road. We camped along the way, sometimes in a stranger's field. We met some kind and interesting people on that journey.

Pamela, who at fifteen years of age had already started high school, was devastated by the decision to move. She cried pretty well the whole trip north, mourning her lost friends and her life at school, and perhaps fearing what she might face in the north. Nell and I, at thirteen and eleven, were less concerned, likely because we didn't have a good grasp of how our lives were about to change. Nor did we have any control over where we were to wind up or what we would do when we got there.

Once we reached the town of Taylor, situated on the Alaska Highway north of Dawson Creek and south of Fort St John, we discovered that when the winter ice left the Peace River earlier that spring, it had taken the bridge out with it. The only way across the river was to drive over the railway bridge. This is how the locals were getting back and forth until a new bridge could be built.

It was hair-raising. Dad maneuvered the car up onto the railway tracks, the truck bed bumping up behind. Between the ties, we could see the river water roiling below us. I remember holding my breath in the hope we would get safely across.

So that is how we arrived in Fort St. John, after driving across on the narrow railway ties high above the flooding North Peace River.

FAITH

Mum and Dad both had a strong Christian faith. Through their tough years of growing up, during their marriage and after, they each relied on Jesus' love and support.

Dad had been raised in the Salvation Army tradition, Mum with the Anglican Church. As a family, we seesawed back and forth, attending one or the other service throughout my childhood. When we attended the Anglican Church, Mum would often give each of us a nickel to put in the collection plate when it was passed. We invariably dropped the coins.

Dad especially loved the music with the Salvation Army, the drums and violins. When training as a lawyer, years later, I was impressed with the service the Salvation Army provided to street people and the homeless. Not only do they run shelters and kitchens to feed the needy, they have volunteers who will attend Provincial Court with the homeless to provide a trained unpaid assistant to speak on their behalf for minor infractions such as shoplifting, dine and dash, or being drunk and disorderly in a public place.

Life was not easy for my parents. Their faith saw them through some very difficult times.

FORT ST. JOHN

The town of Fort St. John was first established in 1794 as a fort or fur trading post for the North West Company. It has been moved to various sites on different sides of the Peace River, depending on whether the river was the main mode of transportation, or new roads had made a different site more accessible.

It was early September by the time we arrived there, and we rented a basement suite for a month in someone's house in town to give Dad time to determine where we were going to live. I remember watching other kids heading off to school down the street in the morning, wondering what would happen with my chance at an education.

Mum and Dad sought out the Land Title's office in the small town of Pouce Coupé. There, the agent was able to show my parents a map detailing where quarter-sections of land were currently available, and they chose one just west of the tiny village of Cecil Lake, some miles east of Fort St. John. Dad signed up, received approval, and our destiny was decided. Homesteading 101.

CECIL LAKE

Cecil Lake was a small community consisting of a tiny log-built Anglican church where a service was held every third Sunday of the month, a large community hall with a kitchen and bunkbeds attached at the back, and a baseball field cleared to the side. There was a two-room schoolhouse, and a Co-op store with a gas service station, where groceries were also available and the post office was located. The area had been opened up for homesteading in the 1930s when many families originally moved there to farm the land.

The community hall was used for every local celebration. Weddings were conducted at the church, and the following reception, dinner and dance would be moved over to the community hall, where every family in the area contributed food and drink.

The first year we were there, Nell and I heard at school that there was a fall dance and potluck to be held at the hall, and "the folks" were playing. I asked whose folks would those be. The answer seemed to be simply that "the folks" would play. Being new in the area, our family attended of course with great anticipation, and "the folks" turned out to be the Faulks, a father, son and daughter who played wonderful dance tunes.

When everyone arrived, coats were piled on the two bunk beds in the back room, and food laid out on long tables set up in the hall. As the evening wore on, the food was cleared away, the tables removed and younger children nestled down to sleep among the piles of coats and jackets on the lower bunk bed as the music ramped up and the dancing began. Little girls danced with their fathers, some of them standing on daddy's toes to be escorted across the floor. Clusters of little boys tore around the hall, chasing each other and dodging between the dancers.

Most of the young men lingered outside in the dark, where quite a large quantity of homemade rotgut was rumoured to be consumed. Chairs were lined up down one side of the hall, and the girls sat in a row. When the boys were ready to dance, they walked down the line with their hand out in invitation, until a girl accepted their offer.

Often they were pretty inebriated before they came in to take part in the celebration. Perhaps that's what it took to work up the courage to enter and engage with the rest of the community. Or perhaps that was part of the festivity that they enjoyed.

There was always a Christmas festival there, with performances on the stage. Mum would write up a skit and Nell and I would be volunteered to act it out at the festival. We also sang, depending on what the festival topic was.

However, we never actually saw the lake itself. It is believed to be named after Cecil Morton Roberts who was the chief draughtsman of the Surveyor-General's branch of the British Columbia Department of Lands in 1910.

Once word spread that a family had arrived with a number of daughters, the young men began to gather round. Pamela, my oldest sister, was at home for the first year of our residency on the homestead, doing school by correspondence or what is now called distance-learning although then it was all conducted via the post office.

One afternoon, two young men arrived at our place to visit. Dad chatted with them outside for a while, then brought them into the house where Mum served coffee. They sat and drank their coffee, smoking cigarettes and dropping the ash into the cuffs of their jeans. They didn't say much, but Pamela had obviously already met them, because she hung in there in anticipation, listening.

Finally, one of them got to the point. There was a dance coming up at the community hall, and he formally asked Dad for permission to escort Pamela to the dance. Dad considered, then gave his consent. A time for pickup was arranged and they left. Mission accomplished.

BUILDING THE HOUSE

During the month of our occupation of the basement suite in Fort St. John, Dad spent his days out on the land he had just secured. He built a small structure which would eventually become the kitchen for the house. It was eight feet by twelve feet, walls and floor made of quarter inch plywood, no insulation. My parents bought a cast iron kitchen stove, wood fired, with a water reservoir on one side, and set it up with thicker pieces of wood beneath the feet to support its weight and prevent it from sinking through the plywood floor. Then we moved in.

There was also a dry sink and counter against one wall. A dry sink has no water supply. It is used usually with a basin in it, and the water in the basin can be poured out through the pipe in the bottom of the sink. Sometimes that pipe leads straight outside. Sometimes, as in our situation, it leads to a bucket under the sink. The water could thus be reused to water the garden, or the animals as needed.

In the kitchen, my parents set up a double bed for themselves, and a single bunk positioned above it for the youngest kids. The rest of us slept on the floor. It was now October and the temperature had plummeted.

Pamela began her correspondence courses, as the local school only went to grade eight and she was past that, and my second sister, Nell, and I began to attend the two-room school in the village of Cecil Lake. The first room of the school was for grades one to four, and the second room for grades five to eight.

On the homestead, Dad was felling trees in preparation for building the actual house, and the surrounding neighbours generously organized a house-raising day. Trucks began to arrive early that morning, and men tumbled out of them, carrying axes and saws. More trees were felled, limbed and dragged to the construction site where the ends were whittled until they fit together. By the close of that first day, the walls of the main structure were about eight feet high, no floor as yet.

Dad dug a root cellar in the middle of the square

of walls, to be used for the storage of produce and canning in the future. Little did he know that when the snow melted in the spring the cellar would always fill with water and Mum would find her canning jars had floated off the shelves and were hovering in the water just below the trap door and ladder used to access the space.

As the weeks went by with all of us living in the small kitchen, we began to get sick. Once we all came down with the flu. Most of us stayed in bed, when not throwing up in basins or buckets. Typically, Dad went out to chop firewood, vomiting into the snow when necessary.

Several of the men kindly returned for more days of voluntary work and eventually the house was completed. The roof was constructed of plywood and covered with a thick coating of tar paper. The plywood floor was installed on top of a grid of logs to hold it up off the ground. There was a short staircase to the small second floor that was positioned beneath the eaves with a window at each end. This would be the bedroom for all the children.

One afternoon, Nell and I were sitting in the half-built structure with our dog, Captain, lying at our feet as we grumbled between us about how we were currently living. Nell was using the small axe, impatiently banging it into a log at her feet for emphasis as we discussed our unhappiness over where we had ended up and why we were still living in a tiny shed constructed of quarter-inch plywood in the winter weather surrounding us. As she hammered away at the wood, Captain rose up and put his paw on the log. The axe came down, slicing up between two of his nails into his foot.

Nell and I were both shocked and scrambled to call Mum. We took the dog into the kitchen, Mum found her mending box, and stitched his paw together, to our vast relief. It healed nicely and the dog was again mobile.

Dad cut the doorway through from the kitchen to the log house on Christmas Eve that year.

SNOW

Snow usually came early. In those days, the girls at our two-room school were required by the provincial Department of Education to wear skirts or dresses to school until the end of October, which is when we were allowed to attend class in pants. But the snow always arrived before that. Hallowe'en was carried out in the snow every year up there. As the road to where the school bus stopped to pick us up was two miles away from our house, it was a jarringly cold trek in a skirt. Sometimes we wore pants under our skirts to ward off the frigid temperatures.

As the snow deepened and continued to fall intermittently over the winter months, it began to pile up and the depth increased dramatically. There were times we walked down the road through snow up to our mid thighs. It could be a tough slog. Our family didn't have a vehicle that could navigate such conditions, so there wasn't another option for us. Dad tried to train our dog Captain to pull a sled so Nell and I could take turns walking and riding on the sled. Unfortunately, Captain was a pretty undisciplined animal. The only way we found to get him to turn around and come back to us was to roll off the sled into the snow. Then he would continue racing down the road, and as he got further away, he would respond to our calls and roar back, pulling the empty sled. We soon gave up on that training endeavour.

The wind could be wicked cold as the snow fell. However, when the temperature dropped lower, the wind died down. By the time it hit thirty below Fahrenheit, there would usually be no wind. The air was crisp and clear, crackling around me, but didn't feel as cold as when the wind blew in slightly warmer temperatures.

The school closed when it hit minus thirty, and the bus didn't run. Dad would listen to the radio every morning and if the school was closed, there would be an announcement sent out to the community. The last thing we wanted to do was walk the two miles, wait for a bus that didn't arrive, turn around and walk back.

After we had lived there for a little more than a year, it seemed to register that a family with school children lived on our road, not just the two bachelors who had settled there some years before. Thus, when the snow plow came through, our road would get ploughed too, which was a real luxury. It was much easier to walk the road after it had been ploughed. No trudging through knee deep snow that day.

Given how often and much it snowed each winter, the clearing of our road only happened sporadically and most days the snow was pretty deep. Our winter boots were stuffed with insoles and we wore several pairs of socks with pant legs tucked into them so the boot tops were blocked and the snow didn't collect inside.

We had a driveway from the road to the house, which had been cleared by felling the trees to open up a path when we first built there. It was seldom used, as we had no vehicle. However, when we had visitors the snow would get packed down from the wheels of the visitor's trucks. But, even then, we didn't walk out to the road that way. Going out the driveway to the road and then down added a good half mile to the trek to meet the school bus.

We had forged a different path through the forest, emerging at the ditch beside our road. When the snow first started to fall each winter, we would plough through, creating a path between the trees to the road. As the winter extended, our feet tamped down the snow to create a useful trail. The snow got hard and the trail, although elevated due to the depth of snow compacted on it, would be easier to walk.

However, in the late spring, when everything began to melt, the trail would get slippery and a bit difficult to navigate. The softened snow crust would weaken, and as we walked we would break through the path every few steps, sinking deep into the snow. We had to forcefully lift our boot out to take another step.

Eventually, it was easier to walk beside the trail in the melting snow rather than stick to the trail and continue to break through the crust and struggle to pull our boot out.

OUR CAR

When we first arrived in Fort St. John, we still had the car in which we had travelled north. That vehicle worked for about a year. However, in the first fall, Mum had gone berry picking with Sarah, a neighbour lady who lived a couple of miles away. They were out in the bush with pails picking saskatoon berries and had several buckets full.

At this time, Mum was pregnant with our youngest brother, Teddy, who was born in early spring the following year.

After a morning of picking, Mum was heading home with her friend. On the way, she parked on the side of the road in front of the Co-op store to pick up the mail. But before she or Sarah could get out of the car, they were rear-ended by a transport truck.

The buckets flew into the air, berries spraying everywhere inside the vehicle. The front bench seat disengaged and banged backward into the rear seat. Mum had whiplash and the baby was knocked about in her womb.

The car was a total write off. The insurance company took the truck driver to court, where he testified that the sun was in his eyes and he didn't see a car parked on the side of the road. He paid a tiny sum in damages, which in no way could replace the car. We were left without any transportation.

Pamela, my older sister, still has the rear window from that car. She always intended to make a coffee table out of it.

WATER

Water was always an issue on the homestead. In the spring after the thaw, my sister Nell and I took buckets and walked to the slough which was about a half mile away. We filled the buckets and carried them back to the house. We would do that several times a day, as often as it took to take care of our home. If Mom was doing laundry, it was pretty laborious. If it was just a regular day, we filled the barrel, the wash tub, the reservoir in the cook stove and brought extra buckets for washing dishes.

We were used to having chores to do, there had been plenty of them back in Duncan on Vancouver Island. But this was different. The terrain was more challenging to manage, the distances more difficult. It seemed there was no hour in the day where some type of work wasn't being called for.

Trips to the slough were required every day. The water was actually quite clean until about mid-summer. By then it would begin to taste slimy. The number of frogs would have markedly increased and the mosquitoes would be popping out of the water in clouds. On top of fetching buckets of water, we would walk the cow and calf to the slough each day to water them. Often we were walking barefoot as shoes were sometimes hard to come by, given we children were all constantly out-growing our clothes.

Once, I remember, as we reached the slough, the cow stepped forward to take a drink and landed her hoof on top of Nell's bare foot. Luckily she was standing on the edge of the slough where the mud was soft. Her foot sank into the water under the pressure and she stood still, waiting in pain until the cow finished drinking before we were able to make it step back again and free her foot.

By late summer, the water in the slough was no longer palatable. Our neighbour, Olaf, had a well which he kindly allowed us to use when needed. Dad would hitch a horse to the stoneboat with a few barrels on it, drag it down the dirt road a couple of miles to Olaf's well, and handpump the barrels full. None of us appreciated it very much. The water was full of sulpher and bitter to drink. But, of course, we couldn't have stayed there without access to water.

Then it would snow. We had a forty-five gallon drum standing upright beside the barrel heater in the living area of the house. At the first heavy snowfall, we would fill the barrel with snow several times a day over a week or more until the barrel was full of water. This water was used for drinking, dishes, washing and laundry. After the barrel was full, we only had to fetch snow in buckets a few times a day to keep it topped up.

Once a neighbour lady had come to visit Mum. As she walked around the small living space while chatting with Mum during her visit, she removed her false teeth and casually rinsed them in the barrel. Nell and I watched in horror. As expected, after the neighbour left, Mum had us empty the barrel and begin the process over again until the barrel was full of clean water. I can't imagine we did this willingly. It took so many days to fill the barrel that, as uncooperative teenagers, we were probably pretty grumpy.

After we had lived on the homestead for a few years, Dad hired a guy with a backhoe to come and clear some trees for planting a crop. In addition, he had him scoop a dugout, which filled up with water in the spring. This worked well to provide water for the garden and the animals throughout the early summer. We also swam in it a few times. But the water was full of leeches, and when we emerged from our swim we would find the blood suckers burrowed into our skin. Removing them was painful.

SCHOOL

The local school had two rooms. When we arrived in Cecil Lake, Nell and I were both in the second room for grades five to eight. To our surprise there were quite a few boys in that class who were fifteen and sixteen years old. Most of them had missed a lot of schooling while staying home to help out on their family farms. They would leave the school year early, in April or May, when the ploughing and planting of the land began. And they would arrive back in class later than the other students in the fall, usually in October, when the harvest was finished. As a result it would take them a few years to complete each grade.

There was no bathroom in the school, but a couple of outhouses were provided, one for boys, one for girls. A third building was attached to the schoolrooms, a teacherage consisting of a kitchen, bathroom and two bedrooms, which had an elevated boardwalk leading to the classrooms. The year my sister and I started school in Cecil Lake, there were two young women living in the teacherage, both having just graduated from the University of British Columbia in Vancouver with their teacher's degrees and about to begin their first year of teaching. The substitute teacher for when one or the other was sick, off on a course, or otherwise unavailable, was the mother of one of my friends. This woman had taught at the school in years past and kept her hand in for when she might be needed.

The children in each classroom were lined up in rows of desks by grade, so one row per grade or two if needed. When we had spelling tests, the teacher would walk across the front of the room with four books in hand, call a word to the first row, shuffle the books, call a word to the second row, repeat. After reaching the last row, she would walk back to the first row and begin again with the second spelling word.

The back wall of the room held a giant row of coat hooks. A line of parkas and scarves hung there, a shelf above holding toques and mittens, with an unruly row of snow boots along the floor beneath. We didn't have the regular lunch pails, but lard pails with handles were commonly used. The student's name was painted on the side of the tin or on the lid, or something notable tied to the handle so the child could recognize their own lunch.

After we had been attending school for a couple of months, the other students seemed to get their nerve up. Nell and I were suddenly surrounded at lunchtime one day by a group of girls who were all asking where we were from. As always, we said we were from Duncan, on Vancouver Island, British Columbia. "No," they said, "you're from England." I guess Mum's proper pronunciation had rubbed off on her daughters. That was not the only time I was asked that question.

One day, in the first year we were there, Dad was escorting us to the bus stop, but we were late. We missed the bus, and watched it drive away before we reached the end of our road. Dad didn't give up. He kept us going. We walked another mile to the main road, then two more miles to the Co-op store and gas station, then another mile to the school. The kids at recess surrounded us, wanting to know how we got to school, because they knew we didn't have a vehicle. Some of them had also seen us approaching from up the road, when the bus stopped and then took off without waiting.

When we said we'd walked, they didn't believe

us. No one walked that far. We did.

A few years after we arrived in the community, another family landed to settle there, a father and his two sons who started school in the same school room Nell and I were in. In the second winter they were there, the father was walking home from the main road in a snowstorm, and must have lost his way. He didn't arrive home, and when a search was organized, he was found frozen to death in`a ditch. We heard the boys were shipped to family elsewhere to be cared for.

The weather was a major hazard, as we were made aware every day.

CLOTHING

When we arrived in the north, I had two outfits to wear to school. One was a pink fuzzy sweater with short sleeves, which I wore with a grey box-pleated skirt that was obviously an adult size, as the hem reached my ankles and the button on the waistband had been moved over several inches to fit my waist.

The second was a red corduroy jumper that I was very fond of. It had ruffles over the shoulders and I wore it with a white blouse. These clothes had come out of the donation box at the church at our former home. By the end of our first year in the north, I had a growth spurt and could no longer wear the jumper and blouse, to my complete despair.

There was a real technique to dressing for the

northern climate. In winter we dressed for warmth. Believe me when I say, you don't forget the feeling of frostbite on your fingers. And once you experience it, you never want to go there again.

Here is how we dressed. Put on a pair of underpants, then a long underwear top. Then pull on long underwear bottoms and tuck the top into them. Then put on the first pair of socks, tucking the legs of underwear bottoms into the top of the socks. Then put on a sweater, then put on pants and tuck the sweater into the pants before doing them up. Then put on a second pair of socks and tuck the bottom of the pant legs into the top of the socks.

When ready to leave the house, pull on your boots with the felt insoles positioned in the bottom. Put on a scarf wrapped around your neck and crossed over your chest. Then put on a first pair of mittens with the sleeves of your sweater tucked into them, then put on the parka. Zip the parka, put on a toque. Pull up the hood and tie a second scarf to cover the lower half of your face, knotted behind the hood. If it was a day of heavy wind, a third scarf might be needed to cover your forehead. Put on a second pair of mittens, tucked into the parka sleeves if possible.

When we first arrived up north, my parents still

had money from the sale of our house in Duncan. We all got parkas, boots, insoles, that fit. But during the next couple of years, the money had been spent and I had a growth spurt so my original parka and boots didn't fit any more. There were times when I wore Mum's parka and her boots for the walk to school, and she was left at home with three little kids and no warm coat or footwear if she needed to go out. It was worrisome.

In the summer, things were different. During the first months of spring there were huge clouds of mosquitoes and during the next two months there were biting flies, horseflies. So, although it was much warmer, it wasn't advisable to venture out without covering our skin, especially in the early morning or late afternoon. We were also short of shoes. Nell and I often went barefoot. We frequently didn't have footwear other than a pair of shoes used for best, and it was just easier to go about the homestead without.

FIREWOOD

Firewood was a vital part of keeping our house livable. It was used for the kitchen stove, which provided for all the cooking and kept the small kitchen warm enough to work in. It was also used for the barrel heater in the main room of the house, heating the upstairs as well.

By this time, Pamela had left home and moved into the dormitories in Fort St. John for the school year. Our family income consisted of the government issued Family Allowance, a sum per each child in the family. Pam now attended high school in person in Fort St John. The Family Allowance was enough to pay for the dormitory fee.

Nell and I shared the job of bringing in the firewood. We took turns carrying in armloads of wood for the kitchen stove. Dad had to split this wood into smaller pieces to fit into the fire cavity and moderate the temperature in the oven. To bake, Mum would use larger pieces to bring the temperature to the level she needed. Then she would feed in smaller pieces to keep the fire at a steady elevation. There had been times when a cake didn't rise, or rose too fast and then fell due to the wrong temperatures.

I remember once Mum opened the kitchen door and irritably threw a cake pan into the yard, slamming the door closed afterward. Playing outside, my sisters and I watched carefully to see if the door was going to open again, because obviously Mum was angry and we didn't want to provoke her response.

When the door stayed closed, we crept closer and devoured the cake, flat but tasty.

The heater in the main room was a barrel heater. Dad had taken a forty-five gallon drum and laid it on its side. He used two pieces of metal, each about two inches wide and several feet long, bent them to act as legs for the barrel, and soldered the legs into place. Then he cut a square out of the top (now the front) of the barrel and added hinges to allow it to be opened and closed like a door, with a metal hook to catch the handle and keep it shut. This was the door to allow wood to be put onto the fire.

Across the barrel's bung hole, he attached a metal piece held in place with a screw to allow the metal to be moved to cover or uncover the hole below the door. This allowed air into the burning fire and helped regulate the speed of burn. Lastly, once the barrel was on its side resting on the legs, he cut a hole at the back of the barrel and installed a stovepipe. The pipe went straight up through the floor of the upstairs bedroom and on through the roof. This heater provided the only source of heat for the house.

The wood for this heater was quite different from that for the cookstove. Dad would chop down a tree, and using his bucksaw, cut it into three foot lengths. My sister and I assisted Dad in carrying these into the house as well, stowing them in the long wooden box beside the heater. Dad would throw them into the heater, one at a time as they burned down. At night, he would fill the heater up and shut the bung hole, usually having to rise once in the night to add more wood.

It was always chilly in the house in the morning. We would rise from bed and quickly struggle into our long underwear and socks, adding a wool sweater if we had one.

Wood was not always in plentiful supply. Most

men might cut wood all summer to ensure a plentiful winter's supply. Dad often left it until we had a strong need for it. A few times he was able to borrow a horse from a neighbour. He would take this opportunity to cut trees in the woods with his axe and drag them to the clearing near our house. There he used his bucksaw to cut the different lengths, some for the heater, some to be chopped for the cookstove.

One winter's night, I was washing the supper dishes in a basin in the dry sink when I heard Dad scuffling at the wooden latch on the kitchen door. I walked over to open it for him. Often, with the leather mittens he wore over wool mitts, it was hard to manage the doors. When I opened the door, he staggered in, holding one mitten-covered hand over the side of his face.

The light was dim, I was working with the coal oil lamp on the counter, but I could still see something dark dripping from beneath his mitten and onto the front of his parka. He took his hand away and I saw a deep gash across his cheekbone. Apparently he'd been using the chainsaw to cut firewood and it hit a knot in the tree, flashed back and caught him in the face. Luckily it didn't take his eye out. It was so like Dad not to say anything or call out for help, but just scrabble to open the kitchen door.

I yelled for Mum. She came quickly, assessed the situation, and dragged him into the main room to seat him on the bench. She got a damp cloth and got him to hold it over the cut, then put her parka and boots on. At that point, we had a vehicle, a secondhand tractor. They hitched a wagon to the back of the tractor and set off for town. Nell and I were left to close up and stay with the younger kids.

Later we learned it took them about four hours to get to town. The old road wound like a snake down over the breaks to the bridge below and across the Beatton River, then back up the breaks on the other side. Luckily the hospital was at that end of town.

Mum parked the tractor in the parking lot which was nearly empty, and ushered Dad into the Emergency entrance. The doctors on duty stitched him up, sprayed a plastic bandage over the wound and sent him on his way. Mum and Dad got back on the tractor and headed home, arriving before midday.

MOSQUITOES

The northern territory of British Columbia is well known for flying insects. During World War Two, when the Alaska Highway was under construction, a lot of the wetlands were sprayed with diesel fuel or other insect retardants from low flying aircraft. The diesel oil rested on the surface of the water and coated the insects as they emerged, killing them. I heard rumours that it helped immeasurably with the numbers of mosquitoes.

By the time we moved up there, the effect must have worn off. During the spring and early summer, there were so many mosquitoes we couldn't sleep without flapping the sheets to ensure there were no insects in the bed, then crawling under the sheet and sleeping with the bedding over our heads, breathing beneath it.

Log houses have gaps or chinks between the logs that are usually filled to prevent insects getting in and to keep the cold out. The chinking we used to fill those gaps consisted of mud with chopped shreds of straw mixed in. The mud would cling to the logs and dry in place, the straw keeping it from disintegrating once it was dry. However, it needed to be replaced every year as the mud would shrink or fall out. That didn't happen with our house.

When the mosquitos were especially bad, Mum would get us all outside just before bedtime. Then she would light a smudge, something that would smoke heavily, in a bucket. She left it in the house until the whole structure was filled with smoke. Then she brought the smudge outside to dispose of it. The smoke travelled through the building, leaking out between the logs and driving the mosquitoes out with it. It was so much more comfortable to sleep after that.

I can only imagine what we smelled like when we travelled to town to visit friends. Our clothing would be full of smoke, not something we even noticed any more. We were inured to it.

To milk the cow in the evening, I would tie a kerchief on my head, put on a long-sleeved shirt and button the cuffs at the wrist. I added a scarf around the lower half of my face and used it to cover my neck and chest. I would put on long pants tucked into socks. Otherwise, I would be badly bitten by the mosquitoes or by the biting flies later in the season.

TOOTHPASTE

Toothpaste, shampoo and other luxuries were things we could not afford when living on the homestead. Shampoo was a bar of dish soap rubbed over my wet hair. Toothpaste was Mum's solution, consisting of a tiny bit of baking soda which I shook into the palm of my hand. Then I wet my toothbrush and pressed it into the baking soda until it glued there. I scrubbed my teeth with the paste.

The first time I saw a dentist I was nine, in Duncan, BC. He took one look at the back tooth that was bothering me and pulled it out. It was so well rooted in my jaw, he nearly had to put his knee on my chest to pry it loose.

The second time I saw a dentist, I was sixteen and my parents took us all to Dawson Creek, to a practicing dentist who was willing to do his work for a smaller fee. No tooth pulling for me that time, just a few fillings.

PAPER

Paper was always in short supply. I am reminded of that whenever I open a cookbook that belonged to my mother. My little brothers did drawings and printed words in the margins and between the recipes, wherever they could find an empty spot.

When we received a letter, the envelope was slit open carefully up three sides and flattened so the inside was repurposed for writing. Stopping at the co-op store for our mail, we would pick up any free flyers there. The margins and edges could be used again.

My children tease me now about how I collect small pads of paper and other scraps and use them for notes. It's not something I have been able to give up. Paper became too precious.

Mum was a poet and wrote stories. She needed paper for her typewriter. Now and then she had the money to buy a pad of paper or a package of it. She guarded it carefully, yet many of her poems I have found hand printed on the inside of used envelopes.

SOAP

Soap was expensive. We never threw away a scrap of soap. When the bar of soap was worn down to the tiniest sliver, Mum put it in a jar of water. The soap would slowly dissolve, and that soap solution was used to wash the laundry.

Two scraps of soap could be sandwiched together to form one piece of soap. Even as adults, my sisters and I have discovered we still do this so as not to waste the soap. My two sisters were discussing it recently. Pamela said, "But it doesn't work," which told me she had tried it not long ago. Nell said, "You have to use enough water." I laughed. I still do that myself.

LAUNDRY

Laundry was a challenge for a family of eight. My parents had brought the wringer washing machine north with them, but we had no electricity. So Dad bought a generator, on credit as it turned out. With gas on hand, and Dad firing the generator, this meant Mum could do all the laundry in one day, including the diapers for Teddy.

That worked well, with Nell and I hauling water from the slough, and heating it on the cookstove. Then the generator was repossessed by the money lender for lack of payments. Back to the washtub. Mum almost always had to do a load of diapers every day. Those of us who were older were left to handwash our own clothes and hang them to dry on the rack that was suspended from a rope above the kitchen stove.

I remember Mum hanging diapers on the clothes

line outside in the winter, and bringing them in at night frozen solid. She swore they partially dried that way. Then she hung them on the rack above the stove till morning to finish drying.

Having a bath was as much of a challenge as laundry. First of all, we had no bathtub. And of course, no easy source of water, hot or cold. To wash my hair, I got a basin of hot water from the cookstove, adding cold to bring it to the right temperature. Then I took a jug and filled it from the basin to set aside. I leaned over the basin and used a cup to scoop water and pour it over my head to wet my hair. I rubbed my hair with a bar of dish soap and sudsed it heavily, then used the cup again to rinse from the basin. Usually a second soaping was required. I rinsed again from the basin to get rid of as much soap as I could. Then I called my sister to give me a final rinse from the clean water set aside in the jug. Leaving soap on the head caused itching, so we worked together to avoid it if possible.

A bath was similar. Usually a basin wash did the trick. Now and then, we carried the washtub upstairs and filled it half full of water. Then I was able to sit in it and leave my legs hanging out. After sponging my body down, I could climb out and step in to clean my legs and feet. Often there was a younger sibling waiting to use the water when I was finished.

WOLVES

There were a lot of wolves around the land. They were curious and tempted by our chickens and geese, our pigs and calves. We had to be on the alert. Yet they tended to steer clear of humans.

One day Mum called to my little brother who was upstairs looking out the window, "Are you okay up there, Derek? What are you doing?"

"Nothing," he replied, "Just listening to the wolves howling in my ears."

When Nell and I finished attending the two-room school and began correspondence, or distance learning as it is called now, our younger sister, Cindy, was in grade two at the school. She was seven and had to be walked down the road to the bus stop. At the end of the day, someone had to go down and meet the bus there to walk her home. Nell and I took turns.

One day, I had walked Cindy down to the bus stop, our dog Captain coming with me as usual. Snow had fallen but the road had been ploughed for us so it was easy walking. Captain was a pretty uncontrollable animal and loved to chase rabbits. Halfway to the bus stop, he took off through the woods yipping away, on the trail of a rabbit. Soon I couldn't even hear him in the still frosty air.

I got my sister onto the bus and turned to head home, calling for the dog. There was a faint sound coming from the woods, growing louder as he approached. He leaped the snow bank onto the road and I called him to come with me. But Captain just kept running full tilt, yipping and barreling through the trees on the other side of the road away from me.

I looked up to the top of the snowbank and two timber wolves had paused there, gazing down at me. I stalled. I actually thought I was going to die right then. So I raised my arms above my head, yelled as loud as I could, and charged toward them. They turned to face the road and leaped down the snowbank, paced across the road and into the woods on the other side, following Captain's trail.

What I noticed was Captain had been panting heavily and running flat out when he ran across the road and into the bush. But wolves have longer legs than a domestic dog. They loped effortlessly across the road at about the same speed my dog had travelled. I expected to never see Captain again.

When I got home, the dog wasn't there. But he arrived about noon, scratching at the door to come in. He settled down by the heater and slept the rest of the day, totally exhausted.

COWS

We always had a cow when I was growing up. Milk, butter, cheese all formed a huge part of our food source. When Mum was a baby, she had a strong allergic reaction to milk products and had to be taken off milk and fed stout to keep her strength up.

I seemed to have a similar reaction to it. Not that I ever had a diet that didn't include these products so it would have been hard to tell. But I had a cold most of the time, a cough with phlegm, and a runny nose. Dad had what he called hay fever, although he suffered from it all year round. So I never wondered why I had those symptoms, simply assuming I had inherited his 'hay fever'. I sneezed often and many things would trigger it. If I looked into a light, I sneezed. If the temperature in the room changed, dropping even a tiny bit, I would sneeze in reaction to that.

We had a hand powered churn. Mum would save the cream off the milk for a week or so, then get the churn out. Nell and I had the job of turning the handle until the butter separated from the buttermilk. Mum even found methods of making cheese with the milk, which turned out to be very tasty.

GEESE

We had raised a small flock of geese along with our chickens. The eggs they laid were about the size of four or five chicken eggs. Mum made all kinds of great dishes with those huge eggs. I have to admit I could never eat a goose egg if it was hard boiled or fried for me. There was something about the size of them that turned my stomach, but they also had a different flavour.

One thing we did was take a raw goose egg, pierce a hole in each end of the eggshell, blow the egg itself out into a bowl for later use, then let the shell dry. We dyed the shell, sometimes using wax to block off areas to protect them from the colour. They could be quite beautiful and it was something we often did for Easter.

Geese can be pretty aggressive birds. They

tended to escape the pen and hang around the back door to the kitchen. When I went out there, they got defensive and attacked. Often a thick stick was enough to fend them off, but I had to be pretty forceful about it or they'd bite. They have a wicked bite with those long beaks.

One year, at Thanksgiving, Mum was deciding what we would have for the family dinner. She suggested a goose, asking if we would be okay with that. We all said *no*, they were family pets at this point. So the dinner consisted of potatoes and vegetables.

CHICKENS

The chickens were more restricted than the geese as they were not as capable of protecting or defending themselves. They were enclosed in a fenced pen, with a hen house positioned at one end. Usually the eggs were laid in a nest inside the hen house, although now and then I'd find an egg in the enclosed yard. All the vegetable peelings were dumped in there and the chickens quickly consumed whatever was on offer.

Hawks and eagles liked to hang around the pen, perched in nearby trees or flying low above it. Not that any of them ever managed to get one of our chickens. The pen was too small for them to fly in, pick one off and fly out, but they always seemed hopeful.

One bald eagle in particular had been hanging

around for a couple of days. I asked Dad if I could use the .22 rifle and he found the bullets for me. The eagle was perched in a tree near the chicken pen, shifting now and then on the branch, and turning its head frequently as it eyed the birds below.

I braced the rifle against the outside wall of the kitchen, took aim, and pulled the trigger. The eagle toppled out of the tree. Later, when I learned how bad my eyesight was, I was amazed that I had actually hit it.

FOOD

Mum was a frugal cook. She used liver, kidneys, brains, any part of the animal she could lay her hands on. She made something she called headcheese out of the skull of pigs or cows. She put the animal head into a cooking pot, added onions, herbs and water, and did a slow cook over the stove. Then she let it cool till the next day. She dug out any slivers of meat from the head and left them in the gelatin which had seeped out of the bones. Then she added hard boiled eggs or vegetables and cooked it again before letting it set.

She could cut it into slices to serve, the gelatin was so thick. I mostly hated it. It made me shiver to take a bite, knowing what was in it. Fried liver was easier to eat, even though it was never one of my favourites.

Dad did the butchering of the animals. Chickens, geese, pigeons, rabbits weren't too difficult. Once Mum had asked me to go get her a chicken for dinner that night. I'd never killed a chicken before but had seen Dad do it often enough. I found the axe by the chopping block and caught a chicken. I held it down by its legs with one hand and swung the axe with the other. Just before the axe landed, the chicken jerked. Instead of severing the neck in two, I cut the top of the head off. I jumped back and let go of the bird. The chicken took off, running in circles until it fell down. I grabbed it, went back for the axe and, with a roiling stomach, completed the job.

But for larger animals, cows, calves and pigs, Dad would lead them to the butcher hoist, knock them on the head with a hammer to stun them, string the animal up by the hind legs and slit the throat. Then he cut the head off and proceeded to skin the carcass, cutting up the meat. He didn't shirk from doing it, and on the day of the slaughter we would have a feast of meat, having gone without for quite a while. But Dad didn't eat meat that night.

He had his own favourite foods, which absolutely included porridge. We bought rolled oats by the fifty pound bag.

He was often the one left in charge of the

morning porridge pot, especially after our youngest brother, Teddy, was born, as Mum was busy with the baby first thing in the morning. However, if he forgot the salt, we all shuddered. Or if he forgot to stir the porridge and it scorched on the bottom, that was even worse, as the scorch taste spread throughout the whole pot. Dad must have been raised on porridge. He ate a prodigious amount of it.

We always had milk, of course, to eat with it, and usually a bag of brown sugar which made most things palatable. But we generally wished Mum would make the porridge for breakfast before we set off for school in the morning.

Mum loved birds and usually had a budgie or canary in a cage. She often let it out of the cage during the day to roam the house.

One morning we were eating our breakfast at the table and the budgie was flitting about the room. Dad was having his porridge in a pie plate, his usual dish. The other bowls were too small for the amount he liked to consume. He would sprinkle brown sugar across the top of the porridge, then dig a hole at the side of the plate and pour in a little milk. As he ate, the gap grew and he added milk as needed.

This morning, the budgie landed on the table

beside Dad's plate. Then it hopped up onto the lip of the pie plate and jumped into the porridge. The porridge was still hot, and the budgie squawked, hopping its way through Dad's breakfast to the other side of the pie plate before flying up to the rafters. We all laughed and Dad continued eating his porridge, unperturbed.

SPIDERS

Wood spiders are a fairly large black spider with long black legs and an aggressive nature. Our house was full of them. Nell and I were often bitten while asleep, so they must have crawled into our bed at night.

If I rolled over on one, I was bitten. Not that the bite woke me. I would simply realize in the morning that I had received a bite. When getting dressed, I would find a swollen spot that was awfully painful and recognize another spider bite. Nell once got a bite on her eyelid, and had to go to school with an extremely swollen spot on her face, red and puffy.

The wood spiders were not dangerous in that the bites weren't poisonous. But they were painful and lasted for several days of achiness, tenderness and swelling.

The spiders were everywhere. Yes, I saw them in the woods. I found them in the firewood that I carried into the house. I found them crawling on the floor or across a windowsill, on the benches around our table.

MITTENS

Mum knitted constantly. If she wasn't making sweaters or scarves, she was knitting mittens. Unfortunately, we tended to lose them. Having them fall down the hole in the outhouse at school was an all too common occurrence. Each of us needed two pairs of mittens to go outside or walk to the school bus. That added up to a lot of mittens.

Going to the bathroom in the outhouse was a challenge for girls, especially when they wore two pairs of mittens. Each time a mitten fell down the hole, my heart clenched. Not that Mum complained. Just that it meant one more mismatched pair of mittens to deal with. And sometimes not enough mittens for everyone to keep warm.

Mum knitted after supper, her needles clicking away. Often when she paused to change hands, change yarn or for whatever reason, she would stick her spare knitting needle through her hair which was usually pinned up in a bun at the back of her head.

Then when she was ready to begin knitting again, she'd be at a loss as to where her needle had disappeared to. If we noticed her rummaging around or standing up to search the floor, feeling around under the cushion on the rocking chair where she usually sat, we'd understand what had happened and have to point out that the needle was caught in her hair.

Mum knitted mittens for Dad, too, but he often made his own pair for outerwear. He had some tanned leather, and traced out his mitten size on it. He cut the leather into the right shape and stitched the mittens on the sewing machine which worked with a treadle. He used a heavy needle and thick thread. At times he stitched them by hand if the leather was too thick for the needle of the sewing machine to penetrate. He wore these leather mittens over a pair of knitted woollen ones.

LIGHT

The light in the house was dim. We had one large window in the main room which let in good light during the day if I sat right in front of it, although the days were very short in the winter. We had a coal oil lantern with a metal handle. In addition, there was a glass-based coal oil lamp with a glass globe, and a propane Coleman lantern that used mantles. This lantern gave the best light. After supper, we would all gather around the table to read or write, with the lantern hanging above the centre of the table. This lantern had to be handled with care, as a heavy jolt could break the mantle, and then the light became poor again. We didn't always have extra mantles to replace them.

The coal oil lantern was usually outside with Dad as he did the chores, and the glass coal oil lamp was in the kitchen while the dishes were washed and supper cleared away.

Nell and I loved to read. If the propane lantern was lit downstairs when we went to bed, the light shone through the holes in the floor. One corner of the upstairs had no floor. Dad had run out of plywood when he was building it, and it was left open as the heat came up through the gap from the barrel heater below. My sister and I would lay on the floor and position our books so that the light fell on the page, and we were able to read for a while before the light went out down below.

Sometimes we didn't have propane and we were reduced to the two coal oil lamps. Candles were not much of an option. They were expensive and didn't last long, or give much light. Now and then, we would use a candle on the clothes bureau upstairs to allow us to find our clothes in the dark morning. Once I was brushing my hair in the light of a candle and trying to peer into the foggy mirror of the bureau when I leaned too far forward. My hair caught fire and my bangs burned right off. Luckily, I quickly swiped them with my hand and that was the end of it. The hair fell to the floor and the fire went out.

The light outside was different from what we had been accustomed to in the southern province. In the winter with snow on the ground, a moon gave enough light to negotiate around inside the house without lighting a lamp. When I moved back to Vancouver Island as an adult, I was amazed how dull the nights were when the sky is grey, which is much more usual here.

But not so in the north. In the winter, there were many days of clear bright blue skies, which meant it wasn't snowing. The sunshine reflecting off the snow just made the day brighter. Only when it snowed was the sky obscured. Even though it was still dark when we set off for school in the morning, and the sun had already set by the time we walked home in the afternoon, in between were hours of uplifting light.

Many nights in winter we saw the aurora borealis, or the Northern Lights. They shone in curtains of violet and green, flashing in the sky. Often the air was so still I could hear the lights crackle as they wavered above us. The sight was exhilarating, making my skin prickle with delight.

READING

Everyone in the family loved to read. A bookcase was built under the stairs on the main floor of the house and was filled floor to ceiling with books. Some of them were The Junior Classics, including stories like *The Last of the Mohicans* and *Tom Sawyer*. We also had books by Mary Stewart and Dashiell Hammett. There was a set of encyclopedias that we brought with us from Duncan. I read them all. We all did.

The library in Victoria, the British Columbia capital, performed a service then, whereby if we wrote them with information about what type of book we were looking for, they would mail some books to us without charge. Once everyone had read the books, we mailed them back and ordered more.

But best of all, we had a neighbour, Dave, an

elderly bachelor, who also loved to read. Now and then, he let Nell and I come over to his house which was directly across the road from us, and choose a few books from the floor to ceiling bookshelf in his tiny cabin. He liked western tales, something we had never seen before. I had heard of Zane Grey, but had never seen books by Larry McMurtry, or Louis L'Amour, our neighbour's favourite author. I gobbled them up.

After a few years of coexisting comfortably, whereby Dave would come over for dinner now and then and stay to play cards with our parents, he and Dad had a falling out and a permanent parting of ways. By that time, however, I had read pretty well everything on Dave's bookshelf.

Nell and I wrote our own stories. We composed our own newspapers. They consisted of hand drawn pictures, interviews with imaginary people, news reports we made up, poems and stories we composed. We both still write to this day.

Mum wrote articles and narratives, and was a poet of some fantastic material. She also wrote stories, both fictional and fact, and sold them to various magazines.

Dad loved to tell stories and I loved to hear them. One such story went like this. There was a scar across the back of Dad's hand and someone visiting asked him about it. Dad told of playing cards in a bar with some nefarious characters. The men were betting on their hands, and Dad placed a bet. His opponent, a guy named 'Whip McGee' was suspicious and pulled out his whip. He snapped his whip around Dad's hand, forcing him to dump his cards on the table. It was a somewhat alarming tale but explained the scar on his hand.

The real story went like this—Dad was taking the calf down to the slough to water it and he had the rope wrapped around his hand. The calf bolted. When it took off, the rope pulled around his hand, leaving a deep rope burn. We all laughed at this, as did the visitor when he heard the actual story. The irony was Dad didn't drink or gamble, and thus didn't spend time in bars or play cards with gamblers, other than games like cribbage at home with visitors.

He could recite long tales of derring-do. He sang songs, accompanied by his accordion and mouth organ, and did a lot of drawing. He was a woodworker and lathe worker, making cabinets and trunks, rocking chairs, spinning wheels, and carved wooden plaques. His navy commander was right—he was good with his hands.

MUSIC

There was always a lot of music in our family home. As before mentioned, we took a pump organ with us on our travels north that Nell and I both played. Dad had an accordion that he played with great proficiency and a mouth organ that he'd equipped with a handmade prop to hold it to his mouth while he used both hands on the accordion. We had a Hawaiian guitar that Mum played, and a violin that I played.

It was like having our own family orchestra. We had friends in town who liked to come out, stay for dinner and enjoy the evening show. Dad often started off with reciting one of his long narrative poems such as *The Wreck of the Hesperus* by Henry Wadsworth Longfellow. We would soon segue into singing, often with musical accompaniment.

Mum loved to dance and so I learned how to play *In the Mood* and other upbeat tunes on the organ and she would coax Dad up to dance until my hands had played it so often they wouldn't work anymore. None of us could read music, but all the tunes were played by ear.

PACK RATS AND OTHER RODENTS

I think it might have been pretty easy for rodents to get inside our house. The kitchen door was a piece of quarter-inch plywood, slightly warped, no doorframe to encase it. The door sagged at the corners and was held closed by a wooden latch. The front door into the main room of the log house was similarly fabricated.

The logs that formed the main room didn't exactly fit together perfectly. There were many spots where a rodent could easily squeeze through.

At any rate, it wasn't long after we'd moved in before we saw the first signs of a pack rat in our midst. We found handfuls of grain in our boots by the kitchen door. We found teaspoons in our boots. The scurrying sound was usually only audible at night. As kids, we quivered in our beds.

One night, the rat sounds were more noticeable than usual in the upstairs bedroom. We called Dad. He arrived with the .22 rifle and the lantern. Dad prowled around with the lantern, as we pointed him to look where we'd heard the noise. Finally he spotted the rodent, which had frozen in place when the light appeared.

Dad took aim and fired. The rat fell over dead. The next morning, we found the bullet lodged in one of the books of the Encyclopedia in the bookcase beneath the stairs.

Regular rats were also common, although not as big or noticeable as the pack rats, other than the amount of feces they left behind.

There were also garter snakes although I don't remember ever seeing one in the house. We saw them often in the woods as we wandered barefoot from house to slough to animal pens. One day I came across a snake on the trail leading to the road. Instead of slithering off into the undergrowth as they usually did, it reared back and opened its mouth, showing its fangs and hissing at me.

I had never seen something like that. On Vancouver Island we had a lot of snakes, all garters of various colours, black, turquoise, orange. We played with them, captured them and made snake pits to put them in. I'd never been afraid before. This time, if I approached closer, the snake hissed louder and rose higher. I retreated, unsure if I'd met up with a rattler. Once I was far enough away I turned and fled on bare feet.

BEDS

When we arrived on the land, we had brought a baby crib, two double beds and a single cot. Once the house was constructed, it consisted of the kitchen and the main room of the house. The kitchen was built of plywood which held the kitchen stove, some shelving for a pantry, a dry sink, and a line of nails near the door for parkas, with a string of boots beneath. Mum kept a lot of stuff in this room, such as urns of butter and milk, storage of eggs as it was much cooler in there. In the winter, the milk she kept in there was frozen solid by the time the breakfast meal came around. She would have to set the bucket on the stove to melt enough milk for our morning porridge.

The main floor which was the living space in the log building, also held a tiny area walled off for Mum and Dad's bedroom. In it they had their double bed, and the baby's crib. When we first arrived on the homestead, Derek, at one year old, slept in the crib.

Upstairs were the second double bed, and the single cot. Pamela, our oldest sister got her own bed, the cot. Nell and I shared the double bed, with Cindy, the youngest girl, sleeping between us to ensure she kept warm enough at night.

When the temperature dropped very low, Mum would come upstairs to spread parkas over the top blanket to ensure we were comfortable. Nell and I had developed our own method of warming our feet. Walking around the house at night ensured our feet were always freezing by the time we headed to bed. Once in bed, we found we couldn't fall asleep when our feet stayed cold.

Here is our method. We would turn out backs to each other. Then I would place my feet against the back of Nell's legs. My feet would slowly warm against her heat. Once I was comfortable, I would put my feet down and Nell would raise hers to place against my legs. It was somewhat uncomfortable, but not as bad as being unable to sleep with feet that wouldn't warm.

As time went by, Pamela left home and moved into the dormitory in Fort St John to finish high school. Then Nell, as the next oldest, got the single cot for herself. That left Cindy and I to share the double bed with Derek, our brother, nestled between us for warmth. He had been replaced in the crib by our youngest brother, Teddy.

GARDEN

Mum had always been an avid gardener, but the northern weather was a different situation than she had experienced in the past. She had to identify plants that came to fruition in a shorter season, and could withstand a sudden August dump of snow.

She planted an apple tree right outside the kitchen window. I don't recall any fruit on that tree, but it did survive the winters.

She grew potatoes, leeks, beets, turnips, other root vegetables that would be protected from errant cold snaps by the earth covering them. She tried for raspberries with no luck, but took us on berry picking trips for low bush blueberries and cranberries that grew wild. She took us with her to gather rose hips in the fall from the wild rose bushes, to be used for winter tea, a source of vitamin C.

Dad built a fence around the garden, as the wildlife enjoyed grazing on the fruits of our labour.

I remember two RCMP officers showing up at our place. They had come to call on all the local residents to warn us about several escaped convicts who had fled toward the north. This happened more often than you might imagine. The locals had no electricity, no telephones, and often no radio access, so the only other way to learn of such information was to see posters on the wall in the post office corner of the Co-op store.

Escapees knew they could go out into the bush and set up camp without anyone being the wiser as there was so much unclaimed land in the northern part of the province. At any rate, the cops delivered their news, and Dad took them on a tour of our place.

One of them offered to let me fire his hand gun, which I did, missing the target. I didn't realize until I was about sixteen that I was very near-sighted and needed glasses. At any rate, then

Mum invited them to stay for supper, which they jumped at. Supper was new potatoes and a green salad from the plants in the garden. I think they were a little surprised there was no meat, but Mum had made a loaf of bread, which quickly disappeared.

WANDERING

There were no signposts, no pathways, no trails on our land. I wandered at my own peril.

One day in the summer, I went out for a walk to gain some solitude from our cramped house, with Captain as my companion. As usual I was in bare feet, and stepped gingerly around thorns and tree roots as I roamed. There were a few early low bush blueberries, a cranberry or two that I picked and ate as I went. I heard an owl hooting and spotted it perched on the top branch of a tree, beside a mess of sticks and straw which was obviously the nest. I thought it was unusual to see and hear an owl in the daytime.

When I'd had enough of my own company, I turned to head back to the house, only to discover that I was lost. I gazed in every direction but couldn't make out any marker that I recognized. Then I tried to decide which direction was north, based on the sun's position. But I didn't have a clue what time it was, and that turned out not to be too useful.

"Go home," I called to the dog, waving him off. "Go on, go home."

As usual, Captain proved less than helpful. He meandered here and there, sniffing at fallen logs and tree trunks before stopping to cock his head and listen intently, gazing at something behind me. It gave me the creeps. When I turned there was nothing to see behind me, and I hadn't heard anything.

So I started to walk. I figured there was a road in any direction within three or four miles. I preferred to find the road closest to the location of our house, given that it was getting later in the day and I was barefoot, so picked what I guessed was north and went in that direction. I walked and walked. Captain meandered along nearby, never leading the way, just sniffing the terrain.

Then I heard the call.

Shortly after we had arrived in the north, Dad had found an old tailpipe from a truck, and Mum got him to hang it from a tree near the kitchen door. She used a metal wrench to bang on the side of it, which worked wonderfully well. It produced a loud ringing sound that carried far into the woods. That was our call to come back to the house. Either she needed us for chores or it was meal time.

Once I heard that, I corrected my trajectory and picked up my pace. I was still a long way out when she whacked it again. With the second beacon, I found my way to the house, no thanks to Captain.

BEARS

We didn't see bears often but we knew they were around. One day our neighbour, Olaf, came to ask Dad if he would go up to his place that night and help him deal with a bear that was tunneling into his granary, seeking the wheat he'd stored there. Olaf had tried to scare it away or kill it, but had no luck.

Dad went up with his .303 rifle and they waited for the bear to show up. Dad was in position and shot it twice in the head. It didn't even stop the animal. He realized it was an older bear and its skull was too hard, so he shot it through the eye and killed it. He brought a hind quarter home for meat.

Bear meat can be palatable, but an old bear is

pretty difficult to eat. The flavour was strongly gamey, and the meat itself was like pellets from a pellet gun tied together with gristle. Not really edible. Mum rendered down the fat and used it to store eggs in a crock for the summer.

Another time a bear had begun to chew his way through the garden. Dad waited up at night and caught him at it. He shot him and hung him on the butcher's hoist he used when slaughtering a pig or cow. This bear was young, probably less than a year old. The meat was delicious and we ate most of it.

Later, when Dad returned to live on the homestead alone, he had built himself a new house. This one was not made of logs, but framed and constructed of lumber. But he didn't finish the structure in the usual way. He wrapped the outside with plastic, and set insulation inside between the studs in a friction fit. He kept the heater stocked with wood and was comfortable enough.

However, a bear found his place and began to stalk it, prowling around in the dark, probably attracted by the smell of the food Dad cooked. Dad's bed was positioned up near the ceiling on a landing built against one wall, accessed by a ladder.

One night, the bear gave up his cautious approach and just ripped the plastic off and barged through the frame into the house. Dad woke to the sound of things crashing and banging around as the animal sorted through the pots and pans and dishes to see what he could find to eat. It took some patience to wait him out. Towards morning, after the bear left, Dad came down the ladder, grabbed his rifle and fired it off through the departure hole. But the bear was already long gone.

OUTHOUSE

Of course, without running water, the homestead had no operational toilet. An outhouse had been built in the yard, far enough away so the odour from the structure didn't reach our living quarters. During the day, the outhouse was easy to access. During the night, not so much.

We went to great lengths to ensure we didn't need to use the outhouse at night. Before crawling into bed, we would all make a final trip out to the facility. That wasn't always enough, and sometimes I would need to go again in the middle of the night.

If there was a full or quarter moon, it was easy to find my way to the outhouse in the night. Certainly if there was snow on the ground, it was much brighter out and any bit of moonlight would allow me to find it. However, I can remember nights so dark, I would walk out in the general direction of the outhouse waving my arms in front of me to ensure I didn't run into a tree on my journey forth.

In the winter, I would come downstairs in my nightie, slip bare feet into Mum's boots, put a parka around my shoulders, and walk out.

Toilet paper was, of course, a luxury. Newspapers were treasured for this purpose. Eaton's store used to send out their catalogue on a seasonal basis and it always ended up in the outhouse.

During spring and summertime, the mosquitoes were a pest and didn't encourage spending much time in the outhouse with bare skin exposed. Spiders took advantage as well. Spider bites on my bottom or legs were not only itchy but swollen and painful.

STONEBOAT

A stoneboat is a vehicle with no wheels. Hard to imagine, right? It is usually made of logs fixed together to form a platform. The platform is attached to a couple of ropes which are used to drag it across the ground, for whatever purpose it is needed. We first used a stoneboat to pick stones from the parcel of cleared land. We used a neighbour's horse to pull it, and we walked up and down the field in rows beside the stoneboat, piling the rocks on until it was loaded. Then Dad led the horse off to the side of the field, unloaded the rocks and brought it back for the next load.

Perhaps that was the original use of such a device, thus 'stone-boat'. At any rate, gradually the logs wore down until they were flat and smooth on the bottom of the platform, and it became easier to drag. We also used the stoneboat to take barrels the two miles down the dirt road to our neighbour's place and bring back well water in the late summer when we no longer had access to clean water at our place.

HORSES

When you don't have a truck or tractor, horses are very useful on a place such as a homestead. Our neighbours were generous souls and they often loaned us a horse when needed. One neighbour had two work horses, called Mike and Darky. Mike was blind, had been for years, and Darky was the team lead. Mike followed along wherever Darky guided him.

We used these two horses several different years to pull in trees that had been felled to cut and split firewood. They also pulled the stoneboat as we picked the rocks off the field. In addition, they were there a few times to bring water from our neighbour's well.

One time Dad had cut down a few trees and had the horses pulling them up to the house. I was riding Darky, holding onto his harness. He bolted, probably because he was not used to having a rider. I was unprepared and fell off his back onto the ground. However, my foot got tangled in the harness, and I was dragged along the ground as the horses headed into the woods. Luckily Darky had slowed, probably happy he'd dislodged his unwelcome rider.

Dad darted forward and caught the reins to bring them to a halt. Then he came to see if I was all right. The truth was, I wasn't hurt, but I had just gotten a new pair of jeans which was an extremely unusual event. The seat of my jeans was now muddy and stained. I was pretty disgruntled.

At one point Dad decided that he'd had no luck with the tractor, which had given up operating, and we should get a horse of our own. I don't know where he found it, but soon a large grey animal had joined the menagerie at our place.

However, it turned out this horse wasn't too healthy. No more than six months after we bought him, he began to grow alarmingly weak, until he could barely stand up. Dad thought he couldn't eat properly and examined his teeth, finding they were badly matched top and bottom for chewing grain. So he filed his teeth down, evening them out. But the animal's health did not improve, and a few months later, he died.

THE PHOTOGRAPHER

One day, after about five years on the homestead, some strangers appeared at our place. A photographer and his driver had come out from town to introduce themselves. This was a professional photographer named Horst who spent his career travelling Canada, recording what he saw. He had arrived in the North Peace area to do a documentary on modern day homesteading for the Canadian national weekly magazine.

When he stopped in Fort St. John, someone he met suggested he come out to meet my family. Horst stayed in the area for about a week, coming out every day to take photos of our lifestyle, our home, and the way we lived. He became a new friend.

He entertained us with his own stories of travels

across the country and the people he had met. He told of taking photos in the extreme north, where his assistants who were local residents, had erected a tent and lit a fire inside so they could all go in to warm up when needed. This was a time of real film negatives, nothing was digital.

As he took photos in the cold, he realized the film was freezing inside his camera and it was beginning to crack as he wound it forward for the next shot. He asked his assistant to take a roll of film into the tent and warm it up. When he followed, looking for some warmer thawed film, he found the fellow had pulled the film right out of the case, and was holding it aloft between his hands to warm over the fire. Of course, it was no longer useable, having been totally exposed to the light.

When Horst discovered Mum was a writer, with permission from his boss, he encouraged her to write the magazine piece as he photographed it. Thus Mum was paid by the word for the article on homesteading that was published in the national weekly that summer. A photo of Mum seated by the corner of the log cabin, Dad standing behind her, appeared on the front cover.

One of the things we got a kick out of in the

article was a photo of Mum dipping a cup into a fifty pound sack of Robin Hood flour as she made bread at the table. The caption read, "They make bread from grain grown on their own land," which of course was not true. Mum got to tell the story, but not to write the captions for the photos, obviously.

The next year, I got a letter from the woman who had been my first teacher at the two-room school at Cecil Lake. She had seen the article featuring our family in the Life International magazine edition while travelling in India and had been surprised and pleased to recognize us.

COMMUNICATION

This was not a digital age. Cell phones and the Internet didn't yet exist. Radios, landline telephones and the postal service were the usual options available. However, where we lived, no landline telephones existed. A lot of letters were written to keep in touch with family and friends. The local radio station offered the service of sending out messages over the air waves.

In addition to letting people know that school was cancelled when the temperature dropped too low, the local radio also had a six o'clock message time to send local information. Once, after leaving the north, I had returned up there to visit family. I sent a message by way of the radio to let Dad know that I was in Fort St John and would come out to see him the next day. That way, he would know to be home when I got there.

Sure enough, when I arrived he opened the door to greet me, but said, "If I'd known you were coming, I would have baked a cake." We both laughed, as this was a common saying he often employed.

I had come ready to stay the night. After he fed me dinner, he pulled a cake off the shelf in the kitchen, already iced. We had another laugh over that. He had certainly gotten the message.

LEAVING THE HOMESTEAD

After many years on the homestead, money had run out and we were having trouble finding enough cash to buy food to feed the family, let alone for clothing or shoes. One evening, Mum and Dad sat us down at the supper table and said they had a decision to make. They had heard of a large farm to the north of Fort St. John with a need for workers. Each worker was welcome to bring his family. Family housing was provided on the property, and a monthly wage was paid to the farm worker.

I thought that made sense. Nell and I had been doing correspondence for a few years by then, and it would be great to be closer to other families in the same position. Not only that, to have a steady wage coming in would certainly brighten things up for the whole family.

My parents wanted to know what we thought. Before I could say anything, the other kids waded in to say they liked living on the homestead, and didn't want to leave it. What would happen to our home if we left? So I closed my mouth, and Mum and Dad agreed with them. We would stay on the homestead and make it work. We would all do what we could to earn some money and remain on our land.

After that, my sister and I did house-cleaning for several of our town friends and families. Mum sold a few poems. Dad worked on the harvest at our neighbour's place and Mum, Nell and I did the cooking for the crew—breakfast, lunch sandwiches and coffee, afternoon snack, and dinner back at our place. It meant a lot of potato peeling, a fresh batch of bread every day, heavy grocery shopping. Our own diet improved during those times.

But overall the income didn't increase enough to sustain the family on the homestead. By that time, Mum and Dad had each made an additional application for a quarter section of land in their own names. They now had three quarters or four hundred and eighty acres between them. Our income didn't benefit from that, however. There was still no farming being done.

Our pastor, who had become a family friend,

came to Cecil Lake on the third week of each month to hold a church service. He had three outlying parishes to deal with, so did a Sunday morning service at the church in Fort St. John, and then an afternoon service at one of his other parishes.

He often came back to our place for dinner after the monthly service in Cecil Lake, and he understood well what our circumstances were. He made us an offer, to move closer to town and occupy an empty house called the Abbey which was owned by the church. It was positioned along the Alaska Highway just south of the town of Fort St. John. The rent would be low, less than for a house in town and we would be close enough to town to get work.

There was a lot of excitement in our home after that offer, and an equal amount of sorrow. Leaving seemed the right move, given our circumstances, but we had made a home there and weren't anxious to leave it.

THE ABBEY

When it was first opened up, the North Peace River area attracted church missions from England. Our neighbours at Cecil Lake told of nursing missionaries, centred in Fort St. John, that travelled around the outlying areas to provide medical and nursing services. Our neighbour, Olaf, talked of once having a dreadful toothache when the nurses came to hold a clinic at Cecil Lake. They examined his mouth, sat him in a chair, took a pair of pliers and extracted the tooth. They stitched up wounds, put splints on broken fingers and limbs, and applied poultices as and where needed.

One of the Fort St. John area early pioneers most famed for endurance was not a farmer or trapper, but a woman born to a cultured English family. Monica Storrs was born in 1888 at St. Peter's Vicarage, Grosvenor Gardens, England.

As the daughter of an Anglican minister, she became involved with pastoral work, Sunday school, and Boy Scout and Girl Guide training back home. While attending St. Christopher's College in Blackheath, England, she met a woman who told her about the spiritual and physical needs of settlers in Canada's newly-opened Peace River country. Monica agreed to go there for a year to perform church services, start Sunday schools and meet with women who might go for months without talking to another female.

Storrs arrived in Fort St. John in October of 1929, as both the Great Depression and winter began. She was the first missionary who came to teach Sunday school and perform regular services, and the first who taught Scouting and Guiding to the children of the area. An 18x24-foot log house was built as her headquarters. It became both a home for her and a dormitory for students from remote farms who moved closer to town for education. By 1934 the house had been enlarged, but had become too crowded despite the several additions, and the tiny Holy Cross Chapel was built nearby, on "the breaks", high above the Peace River. It became known as "The Abbey" and she worked there until 1950, not for one year, which she first volunteered for, but for twenty-one years.

When we arrived at it, the Abbey house was two full stories, with a large dining and living area. The kitchen was an add-on at the front of the structure. Three tiny bedrooms had been built in a row down one side, lining the living area, and stairs led to the second floor. The upper floor had been divided into two semi-detached dormitory-like rooms, one for boys, one for girls. The purpose of the establishment was to bring children closer to town in order to get an education.

At the back of the property were barns and sheds with fenced corrals. The Abbey was obviously designed to be self-sustaining.

This structure did not have running water, or electricity, just like the homestead. But we were used to that. What it did have was proximity to town. Now, I could attend high school in person, and find myself a job.

We moved into the Abbey in the summer. Soon, I was registered for grade eleven in the high school and provided their office my correspondence credentials. I was put into a math class to cover grade 10 and 11 in the same year, as I had started but not yet completed grade 10 math by correspondence. The rest of my classes were the usual. Luckily, there was a school bus, so I didn't have to walk the three miles into town.

Dad thought I should quit school at this point and work full-time to help support the family. Mum didn't agree, and although she thought we should all work and pay board, she supported my wish to continue my schooling.

I took a job at the local Kentucky Fried Chicken outlet as a cook's assistant. I worked one night during the school week and both weekend nights. Again luckily, my manager had to drive me home as the place closed at midnight and there was no bus system available at that time of night. I was so grateful for the opportunity.

Mum began to make her writing pay off. She attended school board meetings and wrote up reports for the local paper—the Alaska Highway News. Ma Murray, a BC icon, was still active at the paper at that time, as well as with the local writer's group which Mum promptly joined.

The high school was full of kids who had come in from the outlying areas to get their education. Many of them bunked in with families that lived in town in order to have access to the school. One student that I knew lived with a man and his wife who needed help. The wife was bedridden and the husband went out every day to his job. This student fed the wife before she left for school in the morning and when she got back from classes in the afternoon. Then she made dinner for the family.

Some families took in boarders for pay. It benefitted the families and the boarders. A lot of the students were older than the usual. In grade twelve, many of the young men in my classes were nineteen or twenty. They did what they had to do, and fit their classes in between other jobs and commitments.

In the summer after grade eleven, I kept my cooking job at Kentucky Fried Chicken and got a second position with a group that was running a summer daycare programme. Now I was working every day, but it was worth it. For once I had money to pay board at home, as well as to buy yards of material to make clothes for myself. It was amazing to have that opportunity, and the treadle sewing machine still worked well.

During grade twelve, I had a variety of teachers. My English teacher was fresh from Wales, with a heavy accent and a distinctly different approach to teaching English than I had been exposed to, including having the students write prose and poetry.

My math teacher hailed from Viet Nam. I had always done well in math but I couldn't understand this man's English, he spoke with such a heavy accent. Even though this teacher kindly offered lunchtime tutoring classes, and I attended them all, I still barely managed to pass the course because his English was unintelligible to me.

My chemistry teacher had taught at the high school for years. But the province had changed the chemistry curriculum that year, and he didn't understand it all. I remember at mid-term exams I had the best mark in the class, receiving 21% on the exam. Things did improve in that subject during the second half of the year.

By the time I graduated, I had chosen to go to art school. My whole family did a lot of drawing, painting, carving and creative work, and Nell and I had decided together to pursue our interests in those activities. We chose the Kootenay School of Art, in Nelson, BC. When we applied, we were both accepted for the fall class.

THE KOOTENAYS

We were on the move again. Apparently, Nell and I weren't going to have this adventure by ourselves. Dad had decided he would attend the classes along with us. After being accepted for the course, he bought a second-hand truck and we loaded what we could into it, leaving many items behind on the homestead. My sister had a boyfriend who had come out from Ontario to work in the north for the summer. As he was already going to drive back home in the fall to attend university, he decided to travel south by way of Nelson before heading east, so several family members were able to ride in his car for the journey.

By this time, Pamela had married, settled in the North Peace, and had a young son. Her husband farmed a large tract of land north of Fort St John.

Thus, we headed to Nelson in September of that year, our parents and five children. Dad's truck often overheated on the drive, so we had to stop at gas stations and put water in the radiator, or once at a ditch where we could access water. We were able to bail it out and fill the radiator. Mum and Dad rode in the front seats of the truck, one child on Mum's lap, and two more of us squeezed behind them. It got us to the Kootenays.

Nelson was a small town built along the Kootenay River, with the main downtown streets parallel to the water. Up the hill to the left were the grounds of the University of Notre Dame which had been established by the Catholic Church years before. Up the hill to the right was the college offering arts and crafts training. Mum and Dad rented a house near the college which worked, as we could easily walk up to our classes. The house came furnished, which was even better. There was a piano, a beautiful couch and armchair set, beds and kitchen table and chairs.

We learned that the home owner had died and the family continued to rent out the house, fully furnished. It performed well for us.

The first job I found was as a waitress at the café in the Greyhound bus stop in town. I worked a couple of nights per week and all the weekends for Mrs. Rivers, who ran the place. Then Dad got a job with a small company that cleaned professional offices in the evening. He brought Nell and me in to work with him, so then I worked more nights.

The Kootenay School of the Arts was a great programme. We got there a few days after classes had started, only to learn the staff and students were waiting with baited breath to see who these three students with the same last name were going to be. To my surprise, there were two other students from my grade twelve grad class in Fort St. John who were also attending that year.

Dad, Nell and I had all enrolled in the fine arts course, a three year programme. There was also a commercial arts course on offer, of a one year duration. My favourite part of our studies turned out to be the clay work, something I had known nothing about. Wheel work, or 'throwing', was wonderful. I had never imagined such freedom. It was like being in a trance. Wedging the lump of clay to ensure there were no air bubbles always put me into the right mood. Just the motion of pushing and rolling the clay was mesmerizing. Then I would plop it on a wheel and begin to form an object—bowl, saucer, plate, vase, and so on. When it was done, I cut it off the wheel with a piece of wire, put it aside to begin the drying process, and started over with a new lump of clay. The next day I would put the forms from the day before upside down on the wheel, held in place by a few lumps of wet clay, to carve and form the bottom or base, then begin the process over again to make new pottery pieces.

I loved it. Then we began to do hand-building, which was much more freeing, and the size of the structure I was making was less limited. I dove into it.

At the same time, I found the art work was not as challenging mentally as I had hoped, and I began to look around for other options. I visited the university and made my application for the following autumn.

Meanwhile, Dad had decided that Nelson wasn't for him. Nor were the art classes, and he made plans to return to the homestead. However, Mum had had enough of homesteading, and living in the house in Nelson with running water and electricity with her small children must have seemed like a real bonus. At this time, my youngest sister, Cindy, was thirteen, and my brothers Derek and Teddy were nine and six.

Nonetheless, Dad had made his decision. He headed back alone to the homestead at the end of the class term in May. Within the month, Nell had left to follow him. As a result, the family was broken apart—Mum, Cindy, Derek, Teddy and I living in Nelson, with Dad, Nell, Pamela and her family back in the north.

BACK TO THE HOMESTEAD

Dad arrived back up north after we had been away for a year. He found the homestead much as we'd left it, although the number of rodents that had taken up residence in the house had increased dramatically. He got a cat and the mice began to disappear. He got a dog, mostly for companionship, but also for protection. It turned out the dog was half German Shepherd, half timber wolf. Dad later told me that if he reprimanded it, the dog gave him a stony stare. If he did it twice, the dog growled at him. He never did it three times.

Dad made some changes at the homestead. He pulled the cook stove into the main room, thus having either the stove or the heater burning was enough to keep the place warm. He moved his bed upstairs, as heat rises. Much more comfortable.

Now that the land title was transferred into his name, proof of active farming or *improvements* were no longer needed. Dad didn't see farming as a benefit. It was a lot of work for very little profit.

He muddled along for a few years, then sold the three quarter sections of land to a neighbouring farmer and bought himself a few acres along the Alaska Highway south of Fort St. John towards the village of Taylor. There he built another cabin and raised a few horses.

If you were to see someone riding north along the highway, or tethering his horse to a parking meter in town, that would be my father. He used to stay the night in town at a friend's place sometimes, leaving his horse tied up in their front yard, until the town council passed a bylaw prohibiting horses overnight within the city limits.

Once Dad qualified for old age security, he discovered the payment was enough for him to live on.

THE AFTERMATH

I did two years at the University of Notre Dame. In my first year, I signed up for six courses. I remember the Registrar having a surprised look on his face when I handed him my form, but he didn't comment. No one had mentioned that five courses was a full load. In my second year, I took a couple of English writing courses and found I enjoyed them very much. But then I moved again, back to Victoria, where I had been born.

During the time I was in Nelson, I worked part-time as well as attending university, and summers I added a full time job to my roster, so I was able to pay board at home. Meanwhile Mum took in a couple of foster children. My youngest sister Cindy was beginning high school, and my two brothers attended primary school up the hill from the house.

Cindy died in a car accident when she was sixteen while learning to drive. She was buried on her seventeenth birthday. I miss her still. She had plans to join me in Victoria when she finished high school. That same year I moved to Japan with my boyfriend and taught English as a second language, before returning to Victoria a year later.

The next winter I was driving up a dark street in the pouring rain when an unusual event occurred. Cindy appeared before me in my car, looking the same as she did when she was sixteen. She was positioned between me and the rear view mirror, seeming to hover in the air. There was no way I wouldn't be able to see her. I slammed on the brakes in alarm. Then she disappeared as quickly as she had materialized. An elderly woman appeared in my headlights, crossing the street in front of me. It was so dark, I hadn't a clue there was anyone there. I was so shocked I had to pull to the side of the street to recover. I would have hit that woman. The apparition saved her life and saved me from an event I would never have recovered from.

Mum moved back to the island with Derek and Teddy a few years later.

Once I had returned to Victoria, I attended university, finishing my BA with a major in

English and Sociology.

I had a number of jobs after that. I managed a night club for a few years, live bands booked every week. When we first opened, the girlfriends of the band members all volunteered to work as servers for the bar.

Later I returned to university and did a doctorate in law, graduating with a JD. During my third year in law school, I discovered that a good friend of mine from my law class was from eastern Canada and his father was Horst, the photographer, whom we had met while living on the homestead all those years ago.

In this way, I was put back in touch with the man who did the homestead photographs. At his retirement, Horst was given an Order of Canada for his lifetime of work, documenting our Canadian way of life across the entire country, and a gallery in Toronto was hosting a survey of his published work for the event. I made reservations and flew back to view the display and meet Horst for a second time.

I had arranged to meet up with the photographer in the afternoon, the day after I arrived in Toronto, so I took the opportunity to walk through the gallery in the morning to view the display. There were photos of many important people from different walks of life in Canada pinned to the walls, but to my astonishment, fully one quarter of the photos in the whole display were of our homestead. It was astonishing to see huge pictures on display of Dad holding little Derek in the air above his head, of Mum mixing bread dough, of Teddy playing with his wooden train, of me milking the cow while Cindy stood beside me telling me her secrets. That one made tears come to my eyes.

As I moved through the exhibition, a group of people came up behind me, surveying the pictures. Then I heard one of the women say to her friend as she pointed to a homestead photo, "That must be Sylvie there, milking the cow."

Startled, I turned around but didn't recognize any of them. Finally, in confusion I said, "I'm Sylvie." They were probably as shocked as I was, and we began to talk. These people knew Horst much better than I did, and as I heard his story, I began to understand why he related so easily to this homesteading family in northern British Columbia.

Horst had been born and raised in Germany and near the end of the Second World War, he was conscripted into the German army at sixteen years of age when their military was so short of manpower. He was captured by the Allies when the war ended months later, and assigned to a concentration camp in France, where he was put to work in a mine. Eventually he became too sick to work underground, but meantime had acquired a camera and began to teach himself the skill of photography.

After release from the concentration camp, Horst emigrated to Canada and began his career as a professional photographer. I think meeting up with a family living on the edge of civilization must have struck a chord deep within him.

I practiced law for a time and enjoyed it immensely, but discovered I fit better in the business world where I managed several night clubs, became an immigration officer, then worked with my partner to buy a commercial building. We started a retail business and leased out the rest of the building to other tenants. The law degree and experience were most helpful in that enterprise.

When I no longer had to work two jobs to support myself, I found time to go back to writing. That is my vocation now—author of twenty books of fiction and several novellas.

****

*****

THE HOMESTEAD

Note to Reader -

I would really like your help. Book reviews are the lifeblood of what I do and your review of my book would mean a lot to me. If you would take a moment or two and leave your review wherever you purchased the book, that would be wonderful. I honestly thank you.

Last but not least, if you find an error in this book, please email me at sylviegraysonauthor@gmail.com . This will help me fix things that my editors and I might have overlooked and make for a better read for others. In return, by way of showing my gratitude, I will send you a free copy of the next book with my sincere thanks.

Sylvie Grayson

You can email me at sylviegraysonauthor@gmail.com

You can learn more from my website at - **www.sylviegrayson.com**
Follow me on BookBub **https://www.bookbub.com/profile/sylvie-grayson?list=author_books**
Follow me on Facebook at https://www.facebook.com/sylvie.grayson/

Legal Obstruction, by Sylvie Grayson

When Emily Drury takes a job as legal counsel for an import-export company, she does it because she needs to get away to safety.

Joe Tanner counts himself lucky. He's charmed a successful big city lawyer into heading up the legal department of his rapidly expanding business. But why would a beautiful woman who could easily make partner in a high profile law firm give it all up to come to Bonnie? As Joe realizes she has become essential to his happiness, his first reaction is to protect her. But he doesn't know the whole story.

Can Emily trust him enough to divulge her secret? And will he learn what he needs to know in time to stop the avalanche that's gaining speed as it races down the hill toward her?

The Lies He Told Me, Book One, by Sylvie Grayson

When Chloe Bowman's husband disappears, never did she imagine that in the midst of the search to find him, she'd discover she didn't really know this man at all. She's left alone with her young son and a time bomb on her hands. Lurking in the shadows is the mysterious Rainman.

Police Detective Ross Cullen was already investigating Chloe's husband when he disappeared. But the deeper Ross digs the less he knows, and the more he's attracted to the young wife as she struggles to put her life back together. Can Ross break through the Rainman's disguises to solve the case so he can be with Chloe?

This is the first time that I read a book written by Sylvie Grayson. The Lies He Told Me is an enjoyable read with several charming characters! There's a lot of twists and turns in this story, and it's also filled with mystery, suspense, and intrigue; all this with a touch of romance!

It tells the story of Chloe, her son Davey, and Police Detective Ross Cullen. Chloe discovered she never knew the man, Jeff, who she had married . . . he simply vanished from her life! That's when Ross, who is investigating her husband's disappearance, enters her life and comes to her rescue. Will he be able to help her? Will he discover the true identity of Jeff?

Together they embark on a journey of discovery, of lies, and secrets. But with spending lots of time close to Chloe, sparks will flare. However, Ross never intended to fall in love with her.

Rain Man, Lies He Told, Book Two, by Sylvie Grayson

Can Rain solve his last case without getting his girlfriend arrested?

Rainier is a survivor. He's made some mistakes, and now he's paying for them. As a condition of his probation, he must work with the police on investigations where his skills might be useful. There is one more case to solve to complete his commitments. Then he'll be free. As he heads undercover to work this last case, Sophia arrives in town. She is a childhood crush who means a great deal to Rain, and she is obviously terrified of someone.

Sophia has made a bad choice in the past, and now she's in hiding to avoid dealing with it. Still, it follows her, and Rainier is the only one she can trust to help her deal with it.

Rain's problem? The clues he uncovers on his final case all seem to lead directly to Sophia. Can he solve the case without breaking his heart or pointing the police in his girlfriend's direction?

Reviewers said—
A story with a great plot. The characters are wonderful and well-developed. Look forward to reading more from this author.

A great read. Thoroughly enjoyed reading it. Good storyline. Captivating characters. Couldn't put it down. Read it in a day.

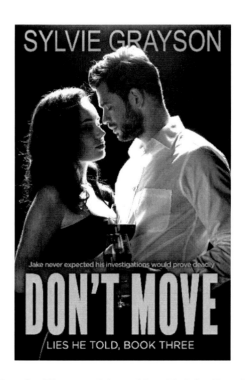

Don't Move, Lies He Told, Book Three, by Sylvie Grayson

Sylvie Grayson delivers another thrilling romantic mystery that will keep you on the edge of your seat— a gripping story of suspense with characters that you'll root for and a plot that pulls you in.

After years of taking courses and jumping through hoops to get licensed, Jake Murdoch is more than ready to open his private investigator's office. Leah Bonnar, a family friend and childhood irritant who blames him for a past disaster in her life, steps in to volunteer as his assistant. Given he's not making money yet, he needs her help to get things up and running. Yet as the cases start pouring in, she organizes the hell out of him. Jake is attracted to Leah, and grudgingly grateful for her help in equal measure. Despite their history, their relationship heats up.

But in the midst of one of his investigations, Jake steps on the toes of a couple of very determined con men and Leah is sitting right in the crosshairs of their revenge. Can Jake find the evidence he needs to stop the criminals, while protecting Leah from their efforts to bring his investigation to a halt?

Game Plan, Lies He Told Book Four

Investigator Randy Bonnar's search for a missing husband uncovers a plot so thick even the cops can't penetrate the secrets in this romantic thriller by bestselling author Sylvie Grayson.

Georgia knows she makes bad decisions. But she seizes control of her future and hires Randy to follow her estranged husband. The facts he uncovers are devastating. Soon Howard's greedy business partners are threatening action if she doesn't stop the investigation, but as Randy digs deeper and uncovers more secrets, they lead in a direction she could never have imagined.

Randy understands his job—protect Georgia—even though it's not clear who or what he's protecting her from. Has the husband left a string of big gambling debts with a determined and violent collector on his trail, or are his nefarious business partners after his share of the investment profits?

When the truth is finally revealed, Randy and Georgia may not survive.

*If you enjoy romantic suspense with mystery, you'll love **Game Plan, Book Four** of Sylvie Grayson's **Lies He Told** series.*

Pick up this romantic thriller today!

Dead Wrong, by Sylvie Grayson

When Shelley's boyfriend disappeared, never did she imagine he'd come back to haunt her.

Shelley Blake is a nine-year-old child prodigy in a sixth-grade classroom when she first meets Chris Wright. He's the big boy in the desk behind who takes her under his protective wing.

But soon she leaves him behind to attend a different school and skip another grade. When she begins university, her classmates observe her extreme youth and walk a wide berth around her. Lonely, she meets charming Billy Zach, but new love soon turns sour. Then Billy disappears.

Years later, Chris appears again in Shelley's life and she wonders if she can trust her growing attraction to him. She's already dealing with her father's worsening emphysema, her sister's secrets, and the demands of her still fledgling business, When the police return, asking questions about Billy Zach, and more evidence is uncovered, Shelley realizes none of it will matter if she's heading to prison for a murder she didn't commit.

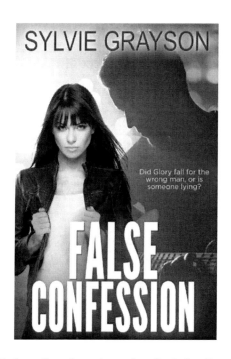

False Confession, by Sylvie Grayson

Did Glory fall for the wrong man, or is someone lying?

Music teacher Glory has given up on men, with good reason. Then she meets the handsome lead guitar player in the band she has just joined.

Alex, body builder and construction foreman, is determinedly single because he's given up on women. But that's before he meets the keyboard player who just joined his brother's rock band. Suddenly his interest is revived and he goes on a crusade to gain Glory's attention.

But when Alex disappears and the police claim they have a confession giving damning evidence against him, Glory must make a decision. Can she trust the man she's fallen for, or has she been fooled into believing a lie?

Well drawn characters. A beautifully done and very well executed plot. Great writing. Yes, this book really does have it all.

This author continues to surprise me with the way I am drawn into her stories so that I feel as if I am experiencing the same world along with the characters. You are in the snowstorm and visiting northern Canada along with Alex, Glory and the band. You also get to see and feel the evolution of a love growing and a love fading. As with Ms. Grayson's other novels, you finish the story with a feeling of having been a part of the narrative as it unfolded. Whatever I read that this author has written, especially the Last War series, I have thoroughly enjoyed.

Moon Shine, by Sylvie Grayson

Some secrets are too dangerous to keep…

A thrilling novel of romantic suspense from author Sylvie Grayson.

After losing her husband to a deadly illness, Julia Butler is determined to look after her family, but this is the 1930's and times are tough for everyone. As the endless string of jobless men trudges past her farm, she does her best to hang on. Then two strangers suddenly appear at her home. They are hiding something that places her family in danger, and nothing will ever be the same.

Dr. Will Stofford has become disillusioned with women. In an effort to heal his broken heart, he leaves his brothers behind and sets up his medical practice in the Kootenays where no one knows him.

Meeting Julia throws his plans into chaos. Will can't turn his back on a challenge and he won't rest until he solves this puzzle and puts things right.

In the 1930's, can a country doctor and a determined widow save the lives of these abandoned strangers?

I really enjoyed this book! It's well written with charming characters like Julia Butler, her two children, Maggie and Jims, and Dr. Will Stofford. MOON SHINE tells the story of Julia, a young widow with two young children living on a farm in rural Canada in the 1930's. It's set during the Depression when men had to wander the roads to find jobs to help their families. These times were rough. However, two surprise visitors are discovered hiding on her farm. Danger lurks around her.

I loved this book. It is well written with a strong female main character and a beautiful storyline with hardship and pain as well as love. I found it hard to put down and read it in one sitting. Looking forward to reading more of her work

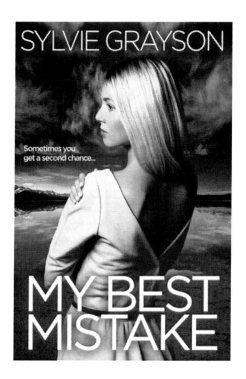

My Best Mistake, by Sylvie Grayson

Sometimes you get a second chance.

Jordie was heartbroken when he returned to
town to find Jenny had married another man.
Now she lives beside him, and he'll either go
crazy or do what he should have done before -
claim her for his own. Jenny is back and she's
angry, her husband cheated and she can't let it
go. But when her boss dies and someone comes
after her, who will she turn to? Can Jordie help
put her life back together?

Jenny has already made a big mistake. Can she risk her heart again, or will this just be another one?

I found this a very intriguing story -- Jenny is a multi-layered clever woman who is trying to put her life back together after a bad divorce. Yes, she's made some mistakes, but as things progress, she's determined not to make the same ones again. She's afraid that Jordie might be one of those mistakes. Her job is to patch her life back together. Well written with lots of action and great characters. I'm looking for Grayson's next book.

Suspended Animation, by Sylvie Grayson

Be careful who you trust...

Katy Dalton worked hard to save her money. And letting her friend Bruno invest it seemed like a safe bet. But her job disappears and she needs her money back, everything Bruno has already loaned to Rome Trucking. When Katy insists he return her money, Bruno stops answering his phone and bad things start to happen.

Brett Rome is frustrated. The last thing he

wants to do is leave a promising career in hockey to come home and run his ailing father's trucking company. What he discovers is not the successful business that he remembers, but one that is teetering on the very edge of bankruptcy and a young woman demanding the return of the money she invested.

With the company in chaos, Brett hires her. But danger lurks in the form of Bruno's dubious associates. What secret are they hiding and why are they willing to kill Katy? Can Brett put this broken picture back together, and is Katy part of the solution or the problem?

A thrilling roller coaster of a story… Interesting characters, family conflicts and divided loyalties make this a book that kept me up half the night. Brett Rome is a hockey player with a bright future called home when his father has a heart attack. Worse, the company is in serious financial trouble. Katy Dalton reminds me of Shelley Long on Cheers although she's brunette, not blonde. She arrives at Rome Trucking searching for money she's 'invested' through a friend

Sylvie Grayson has found her niche, you'll love this book

Fantasy/military thriller from Sylvie Grayson

Aqatain, The Last War Prequel, by Sylvie Grayson

Aqatain the First created an empire. Is Aqatain the Second about to destroy it?

A stunning prequel to the popular Last War series from best-selling author Sylvie Grayson.

Second waited years to take his father's place as Emperor. Now he'll rule the territories his way. He has a son with his mistress.

A son with his wife. His own hareem, and his own army. He's convinced he can do anything he wants.

Then he encounters Jenna, a counsellor's daughter, and immediately falls into lust. Why can't he have her too? After all, he's the Emperor. But General Romero Regiment spotted Jenna at the same time, and determines to pursue his interest. Jenna, however, has plans of her own. She meets Sergeant Ryall Norcross of the empire military and the two fall in love. With determination, Norcross sets out to make her his own. He soon finds himself in opposition to his own commanding officer, and the supreme ruler of the Empire.

Second has a bevy of counsellors to obey his orders and help manage the empire, none of whom dare to question his demands. So as he sets out to capture Jenna, what could possibly go wrong? Yet, when rebellion arises south of Headquarters, his rage knows no limits. As the insurgency gains support throughout the Empire, it swiftly heads out of control. Second has to set aside his other interests to his military into war. Will he be able to save his father's Empire, or is it already too late?

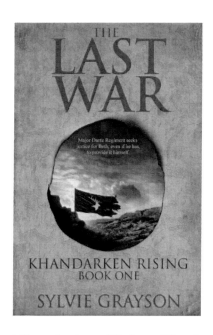

Khandarken Rising, The Last War, Book One, by Sylvie Grayson

The Emperor has been defeated. New countries have arisen from the ashes of the old Empire. The citizens swear they will never need to fight again after that long and painful war.

Bethlehem Farmer is helping her brother Abram run Farmer Holdings in south Khandarken after their father died in the final battles. She is looking after the dispossessed, keeping the farm productive and the talc mine working in the hills behind their land. But when Abram takes a trip with Uncle Jade into the northern territory and disappears without a trace, she's left on her own. Suddenly things are not what they seem and no one can be trusted.

Major Dante Regiment is sent by his father, the General of Khandarken, to find out what the situation is at Farmer Holdings. What he sees shakes him to the core and fuels his grim determination to protect Bethlehem at all cost, even with his life.

Ms Grayson has created a fascinating new world with a lot of the same old problems. Sci fi and fantasy rolled into one with a sure hand and enormous imagination

I couldn't help but think a feeling of deja vu. Like I had heard this story before or like it reminded me of something. And then it hit me. It sounded similar to the fall of the Ottoman Empire after WW1. The new countries that came forth. The battles. The new rulers and emperors fighting to keep their territory. And the citizens, adjusting to the new normal.

And then I realized that this story is one of a kind. It has so many unique characteristics-personal relationships are intriguing, names are cool, the plot gets thicker with each page, and I loved the author's style. It became evident that I was addicted to reading the book. I'm going to give this a strong recommendation. It's my kind of book.

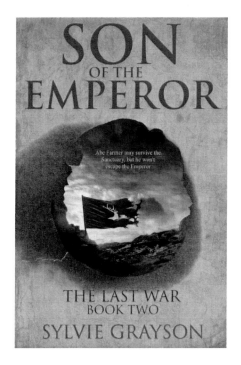

Son of the Emperor, The Last War, Book Two, by Sylvie Grayson

From the mud and danger of the open road to the welcoming arms of the Sanctuary, from attacks by the dispossessed army to the storms of the open sea, Son of the Emperor takes us on a wild ride into danger and on to the dream of freedom.

The Emperor is defeated yet already unrest is growing in the north of Khandarken. After Julianne Adjudicator's father disappears, she seeks to escape the clutches of her vicious stepmother Zanata, and flees to the Sanctuary. This is the safest place for a woman in a hostile world of unrest and roving dispossessed. But when Julianne seeks asylum, it soon becomes clear all is not as it first appeared.

Then Abe Farmer arrives at the Sanctuary seeking medical help. Abe isn't interested in taking a young woman with them, as he and his injured bodyguard struggle to return to the Southern Territory. Yet when he discovers her fate if she stays, he finds he has no choice.

But the journey becomes more dangerous as they encounter the army of the New Emperor and are caught in the middle of a firefight as they flee toward the Catastrophic Ocean. Can Abe keep her safe till they reach home?

...a whole new world with the same old problems - fantasy at its best...

Really a powerful portrayal of how a society deals with massive upheaval - and at the same time a great adventure filled with action, thrills and even romance. Sylvie Grayson really knows how to tell a powerful tale. Strong plot, string characters that readers get invested in. Amazingly strong world-building. What more could one ask for? Enjoy.

Truth and Treachery, The Last War: Book Three
By Sylvie Grayson

When Emperor Carlton makes an offer to Cownden Lanser, can he refuse? Lanser has his own ambitions and Carlton may be offering everything he's dreamed of.

The Young Emperor has been backed into a corner. He holds a bit of land in Legitamia where he marshals his troops, but the skirmishes they've launched to expand his empire have had limited success. Now, his ambitions are aimed at overthrowing everything Khandarken has cobbled together since the Last War.

Cownden Lanser, Chief Constable of Khandarken, is a private man with a close connection to the Old Empire that he doesn't divulge to anyone. Although he's dedicated to his position, things are not what they seem in the rank and file of the police.

Selanna Nettles is a sookie, trained in Legitamia but working near her family in the Western Territory, healing the mine workers. But her life takes a startling turn when Chief Cownden Lanser hires her to attend a set of high-level meetings.

When these three meet up in Legitamia, the result is explosive. Not just for them but for the future of Khandarken. The Emperor makes Cownden an offer that might be everything he's secretly dreamed of. How can he refuse?

The Last War series is a stunning portrayal of a new world created from fire and consumed at the edges… sci fi/fantasy at its best…

Ok, this series is just getting better and better. The increasing complexity of the characters and the development of lead characters is a pleasure to read. The plot, with its twists and turns, intrigue and adventure, is a real joy. If you liked the first two books in The Last War series (and, seriously, that's the place to start before reading this book - it's worth doing) then you will love this book

Weapon of Tyrants, The Last War: Book Four, By Sylvie Grayson

Fanny Master is running for her life. Can she trust a criminal enforcer to keep her safe?

The International Head Balls Games are about to begin at Deep Creek. Tension rises with Adar Silva, Khandarken, Jiran and Legitamia scheduled to take part. Damian Stuke, an enforcer for a gamer in the Western Territory, still has nightmares about being captured and tortured during the Last War. When his sister marries the Chief Constable of Khandarken, his life has to change.

Training for undercover work in Deep Creek in the midst of the Games, he encounters a fascinating woman with a small child and a hidden agenda. But as he discovers what she's hiding, his protective instincts kick into high gear.

Fanny Master's her parents are assassinated, and she runs for her life. A member of the Khandarken elite, she doesn't know who is after he, but she'll do almost anything to remain under the radar. That could include using someone else's ident and adopting their child, a child who might be from another world.

As Emperor Carlton ramps up his plans for invasion, the assassin makes a new attempt on Fanny's life. Damian is her only hope. Will he save her from her unknown enemy, or is he still working for the other side?

The Last War has been a truly excellent series so far, and Weapon of Tyrants is staying strong. Exciting, full of intrigue and adventure, wonderfully developed strong lead characters with a great supporting cast, neat world-building and excellent writing. I mean, what more can you ask for? You do need to start with book 1, but it too was excellent so you can't go wrong, and I can guarantee you'll have a ball with this one.

Find Sylvie Grayson at www.sylviegrayson.com to subscribe to her newsletter

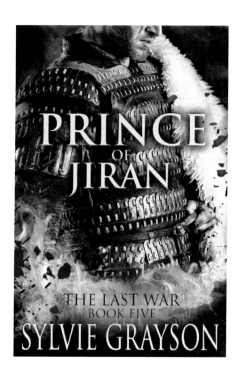

Prince of Jiran, The Last War: Book Five, by Sylvie Grayson

A Penrhy prince caught between duty and desire. Can he win the impending battle?

Shandro, Prince of the Penrhy tribe of Jiran, has a goal to uphold the family values in spite of his father's conniving moves as he deals with the hotbed of competing nations surrounding them.

Then he's is sent on a mission across the mountains into Khandarken to bring back Princess Chinata, a bride for

Emperor Carlton's Advisor. In exchange, Jiran and the Penrhy tribe are given a peace agreement, protection against invasion by the Emperor's troops. This seems a good trade, as Carlton is hovering on their borders with his need for more land. However, not far into the journey, it becomes apparent someone is not adhering to the terms of the peace accord.

Near the tribal border, Shandro and his troops have come under direct attack from unknown forces. He digs deeper into Chinata's background to find strong ties to the New Empire. Is it too dangerous to bring Princess Chinata into Jiran? Or as her escort, does Shandro become her defender against the Emperor's troops?

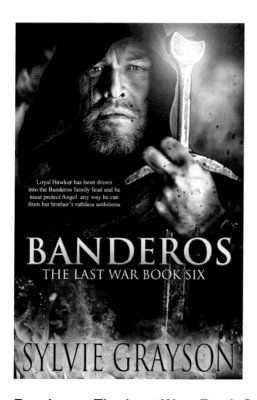

Banderos, The Last War: Book Seven
By Sylvie Grayson

Loyal Hawker must protect Angel any way he can from her brothers' ruthless ambitions.

Loyal Hawker, an undercover agent for the Khandarken military, has never met anyone quite like the woman he encounters on his trip to the south. He's approached by Angel, only daughter among the many sons of Gerwal Banderos, a well-known strongman who seized much of the unclaimed territory north of Adar Silva at the end of the Last War. Angel declares her father wants to meet with him on a matter of urgency. While suspicious of her intentions as she leads him across extensive territory toward the Banderos compound, Loyal can't deny his attraction to her.

With Emperor Carlton invading in an attempt to reclaim his Empire, danger hovers over the Banderos land, and the brothers show they're not as united as they first appear. During the ensuing chaos, when the compound is besieged, Loyal must work in the midst of deceit and betrayal to protect what is left of Angel's heritage. Can he survive long enough to find out who's targeting Angel and save her from her treacherous brothers?

I was hooked with the first book, Khandarken Rising, The Last War: Book One, and will continue to read each subsequent novel. The action is continuous from the beginning thru the end of each book. In addition to a fine story in a differing world, with succinct writing, there are also supernatural incidences that pop up throughout the series that add just a touch of spice. Five stars. Amazon reader.

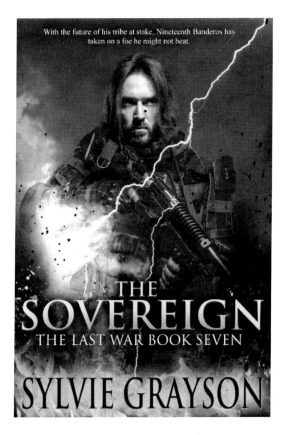

With the future of his tribe at stake, Nineteenth Banderos has taken on a foe he might not beat.

THE SOVEREIGN
THE LAST WAR BOOK SEVEN
SYLVIE GRAYSON

The Sovereign, The Last War: Book Seven by Sylvie Grayson

With the future of his tribe at stake, Nineteenth Banderos has taken on a foe he might not beat.

The ever menacing Emperor has overtaken the city of Sommerset, the seat of power from the Old Empire. Now he's been approached by a local strongman, offering to work with him to seize the Banderos territory.

Nineteenth Banderos has been given the task of heading up a Foreign Legion for the dispossessed, but his plans take a detour when he meets the Shafoneur Sovereign who has plans of his own. Nineteenth isn't one to turn down a challenge, especially if the reward might include the chance to marry a beautiful young Shafoneur girl he's fallen for.

Unfortunately, a war with Emperor Carlton looms on the horizon. Allied with the Shafoneur tribe, Nineteenth is not about to let a neighbour claim their land, but that is not the only threat he faces. Can Nineteenth protect his family and his new alliance?

ABOUT THE AUTHOR

Sylvie Grayson has published a number of contemporary romantic suspense novels, all about strong women who meet with dangerous odds, stories of tension and attraction.

She has also written *The Last War* series, a military thriller and romantic suspense series set in a new world she has created.

She has been an English language instructor, a nightclub manager, an auto shop bookkeeper and a lawyer. She has lived in various spots in British Columbia, Canada, for most of her life, and spent a year in Tokyo, Japan. She is a wife and mother, and lives in southern British Columbia with her husband on a small piece of land near the Pacific Ocean that they call home, when she's not travelling the world looking for adventure.

Follow Sylvie on her website,
www.sylviegrayson.com to read her blog, see
her booklist or new releases,

or email her at   sylviegraysonauthor@gmail.com

Find her on Facebook,
https://www.facebook.com/sylvie.grayson

On BookBub
https://www.bookbub.com/profile/sylvie-grayson?list=about

Manufactured by Amazon.ca
Acheson, AB